Alternative Therapies

Other Books in the Current Controversies Series

Anger Management

Assisted Suicide

Disaster Response

Family Violence

Homeland Security

Homeschooling

Human Trafficking

Media Ethics

The Rights of Animals

Smoking

Vaccines

Alternative Therapies

Debra A. Miller, Book Editor

GREENHAVEN PRESS
A part of Gale, Cengage Learning

Detroit • New York • San Francisco • New Haven, Conn • Waterville, Maine • London

Christine Nasso, *Publisher*
Elizabeth Des Chenes, *Managing Editor*

For more information, contact:
Greenhaven Press
27500 Drake Rd.
Farmington Hills, MI 48331-3535
Or you can visit our Internet site at gale.cengage.com

Articles in Greenhaven Press anthologies are often edited for length to meet page requirements. In addition, original titles of these works are changed to clearly present the main thesis and to explicitly indicate the author's opinion. Every effort is made to ensure that Greenhaven Press accurately reflects the original intent of the authors. Every effort has been made to trace the owners of copyrighted material.

LIBRARY OF CONGRESS CATALOGING-IN-PUBLICATION DATA

Alternative therapies / Debra A. Miller, book editor.
p. cm. -- (Current controversies)
Includes bibliographical references and index.
ISBN 978-0-7377-4128-5 (hardcover)
ISBN 978-0-7377-4129-2 (pbk.)
1. 1. Alternative medicine. I. I. Miller, Debra A.
R733.A515 2009
615.5--dc22
2008020841

Printed in the United States of America
1 2 3 4 5 6 7 12 11 10 09 08

Contents

Chapter 2: Are Alternative Therapies Safe?

Foreword

By definition, controversies are "discussions of questions in which opposing opinions clash" (Webster's Twentieth Century Dictionary Unabridged). Few would deny that controversies are a pervasive part of the human condition and exist on virtually every level of human enterprise. Controversies transpire between individuals and among groups, within nations and between nations. Controversies supply the grist necessary for progress by providing challenges and challengers to the status quo. They also create atmospheres where strife and warfare can flourish. A world without controversies would be a peaceful world; but it also would be, by and large, static and prosaic.

The Series' Purpose

The purpose of the *Current Controversies* series is to explore many of the social, political, and economic controversies dominating the national and international scenes today. Titles selected for inclusion in the series are highly focused and specific. For example, from the larger category of criminal justice, *Current Controversies* deals with specific topics such as police brutality, gun control, white collar crime, and others. The debates in *Current Controversies* also are presented in a useful, timeless fashion. Articles and book excerpts included in each title are selected if they contribute valuable, long-range ideas to the overall debate. And wherever possible, current information is enhanced with historical documents and other relevant materials. Thus, while individual titles are current in focus, every effort is made to ensure that they will not become quickly outdated. Books in the *Current Controversies* series will remain important resources for librarians, teachers, and students for many years.

In addition to keeping the titles focused and specific, great care is taken in the editorial format of each book in the series. Book introductions and chapter prefaces are offered to provide background material for readers. Chapters are organized around several key questions that are answered with diverse opinions representing all points on the political spectrum. Materials in each chapter include opinions in which authors clearly disagree as well as alternative opinions in which authors may agree on a broader issue but disagree on the possible solutions. In this way, the content of each volume in *Current Controversies* mirrors the mosaic of opinions encountered in society. Readers will quickly realize that there are many viable answers to these complex issues. By questioning each author's conclusions, students and casual readers can begin to develop the critical thinking skills so important to evaluating opinionated material.

Current Controversies is also ideal for controlled research. Each anthology in the series is composed of primary sources taken from a wide gamut of informational categories including periodicals, newspapers, books, U.S. and foreign government documents, and the publications of private and public organizations. Readers will find factual support for reports, debates, and research papers covering all areas of important issues. In addition, an annotated table of contents, an index, a book and periodical bibliography, and a list of organizations to contact are included in each book to expedite further research.

Perhaps more than ever before in history, people are confronted with diverse and contradictory information. During the Persian Gulf War, for example, the public was not only treated to minute-to-minute coverage of the war, it was also inundated with critiques of the coverage and countless analyses of the factors motivating U.S. involvement. Being able to sort through the plethora of opinions accompanying today's major issues, and to draw one's own conclusions, can be a complicated and frustrating struggle. It is the editors' hope that *Current Controversies* will help readers with this struggle.

Introduction

> *"CAM therapies . . . encompass a wide variety of health treatments that are considered alternative because they are not yet a part of the body of scientifically proven treatments used in Western medicine—typically surgery and prescription drugs."*

One of the most significant health trends in the United States is the increasing use of alternative health therapies—often called complementary and alternative medicine, or CAM. According to a 2004 survey conducted by the National Center for Complementary and Alternative Medicine (NCCAM), a government-funded agency that is part of the National Institutes of Health (NIH), 36 percent of all Americans use some form of CAM on a regular basis. Other government studies suggest that about one-half of all Americans may have tried alternative therapies at some point in their lives. Baby boomers—people born between 1946 and 1964—are the most likely to try alternative medicine. A 2006 survey by the American Association of Retired Persons (AARP) found that nearly 70 percent of boomers have tried CAM.

The most common alternative treatment appears to be vitamin and herb supplements, which are used by about one-fifth of U.S. adults. The most popular supplements tend to be echinacea (an herb touted as an immunity-booster), ginseng (an herb associated with increased energy and stamina), ginkgo bilboa (an herb linked with memory improvement), and garlic (an herb believed to be a blood thinner and anti-cholesterol agent). Other highly popular alternative therapies used by Americans include meditation, yoga, and massage.

CAM therapies, however, encompass a wide variety of health treatments that are considered alternative because they are not yet a part of the body of scientifically proven treatments used in Western medicine—typically surgery and prescription drugs. Therapies that fall into the CAM category therefore include not only dietary supplements, yoga, massage, and meditation, but also a long list of other treatments. These include chiropractic therapy (spinal manipulation); acupuncture (stimulation of points on the body with thin needles); homeopathy (using minute quantities of various substances to heal illnesses energetically); and naturopathy (whole-body medicine that emphasizes restoring the body's overall health rather than treating disease). Other CAM therapies include aromatherapy (use of essential aromatic plant oils to improve health); traditional Chinese medicine (based on balancing yin and yang forces in the body); and energy healing (a spiritual treatment akin to the religious "laying on of hands").

Some people use CAM therapies along with conventional medicine. Studies have shown, for example, that people recovering from cancer may find acupuncture helpful in relieving surgery-related pain and nausea resulting from chemotherapy. Other people seek out alternative therapies because conventional medicine has failed to provide them with reduction of pain or relief from chronic medical conditions. Chiropractic and massage are CAM therapies that have shown some ability to help reduce the pain of common and sometimes chronic musculoskeletal back and neck conditions. Still others believe that alternative treatments are more "natural" and potentially safer than the prescription drugs typically prescribed by Western doctors. And for a significant number of people, alternative therapies are simply a way to enhance their vitality and live a more healthful, longer, and active life.

Not surprisingly, CAM therapies are now big business. Some estimates indicate that Americans spend $14 billion a year just on vitamins and other supplements, and the total amount spent for all alternative therapies is many times that amount. As alternative treatments become more lucrative, and are demanded by more patients, the Western medical establishment has begun to take notice. Medical schools have started to incorporate CAM therapies in their programs, and some doctors sell supplements and even recommend certain alternative treatments, such as massage, chiropractic, and acupuncture. In addition, a few hospitals are now offering select alternative therapies as part of their care facilities. Most CAM therapies, however, are not yet covered by insurance or by Medicaid or Medicare.

Commentators claim that the future for alternative medicine looks bright, depending on what actions the government takes to regulate the industry. As the huge baby boomer generation ages, medical needs are only going to increase, and this will likely create an ever-growing demand for CAM therapies. Already, women in this age group who are going through menopause are seeking out alternative treatments for hot flashes and related menopausal symptoms. However, many medical experts and consumers worry that most alternative therapies have not been scientifically proven to be either safe or effective, and this has led to a push for more research and more government oversight.

Currently, supplements and other CAM therapies are not regulated by the U.S., but Congress created and funded the NCAAM in 1998 to study the effectiveness of these practices and products and make recommendations to the government. Recently, NCAAM has suggested that more regulation is necessary, especially in the area of dietary supplements, and the U.S. Food and Drug Administration (FDA) has proposed guidelines for how it might classify CAM therapies, most probably in preparation for eventual regulatory action.

Unless and until alternative therapies are restricted or regulated like conventional medical products and services, however, the burden is on consumers to evaluate their safety, effectiveness, and value. The various authors in *Current Controversies: Alternative Therapies* help to provide information about CAM therapies, the critical issues of their safety and effectiveness, and whether action should be taken by the government to regulate their use.

CHAPTER 1

What Are Alternative Therapies?

Chapter Overview

National Center for Complementary and Alternative Medicine

The National Center for Complementary and Alternative Medicine, part of the National Institutes of Health, is the federal government's lead agency for scientific research on complementary and alternative medicine.

There are many terms used to describe approaches to health care that are outside the realm of conventional medicine as practiced in the United States. This [overview] explains how the National Center for Complementary and Alternative Medicine (NCCAM), a component of the National Institutes of Health, defines some of the key terms used in the field of complementary and alternative medicine (CAM). . . .

What Is CAM?

CAM is a group of diverse medical and health care systems, practices, and products that are not presently considered to be part of conventional medicine. Conventional medicine is medicine as practiced by holders of M.D. (medical doctor) or D.O. (doctor of osteopathy) degrees and by their allied health professionals, such as physical therapists, psychologists, and registered nurses. Some health care providers practice both CAM and conventional medicine. While some scientific evidence exists regarding some CAM therapies, for most there are key questions that are yet to be answered through well-designed scientific studies—questions such as whether these therapies are safe and whether they work for the diseases or medical conditions for which they are used. The list of what is considered to be CAM changes continually, as those therapies

National Center for Complementary and Alternative Medicine, "Energy Medicine: An Overview," National Center for Complementary and Alternative Medicine, March 2007. http://nccam.nih.gov/health/whatiscam/#4.

that are proven to be safe and effective become adopted into conventional health care and as new approaches to health care emerge.

Complementary medicine is used together with conventional medicine ... [while] alternative medicine is used in place of conventional medicine.

Are complementary medicine and alternative medicine different from each other? Yes, they are different. Complementary medicine is used together with conventional medicine. An example of a complementary therapy is using aromatherapy. A therapy in which the scent of essential oils from flowers, herbs, and trees is inhaled to promote health and well-being, to help lessen a patient's discomfort following surgery. Alternative medicine is used in place of conventional medicine. An example of an alternative therapy is using a special diet to treat cancer instead of undergoing surgery, radiation, or chemotherapy that has been recommended by a conventional doctor.

What is integrative medicine? Integrative medicine combines treatments from conventional medicine and CAM for which there is some high-quality evidence of safety and effectiveness. It is also called integrated medicine. . . .

Whole Medical Systems

NCCAM groups CAM practices into four domains, recognizing there can be some overlap. In addition, NCCAM studies CAM whole medical systems, which cut across all domains.

Whole medical systems are built upon complete systems of theory and practice. Often, these systems have evolved apart from and earlier than the conventional medical approach used in the United States. Examples of whole medical systems that have developed in Western cultures include homeopathic medicine—a whole medical system that originated in Europe. Homeopathy seeks to stimulate the body's ability to heal itself by giving very small doses of highly diluted substances that in larger doses would produce illness or symptoms (an approach called "like cures like"). . . .

[Another whole medical system is] naturopathic medicine—a whole medical system that originated in Europe. Naturopathy aims to support the body's ability to heal itself through the use of dietary and lifestyle changes together with CAM therapies such as herbs, massage, and joint manipulation.

Examples of systems that have developed in non-Western cultures include traditional Chinese medicine—a whole system that originated in China. It is based on the concept that disease results from disruption in the flow of qi [chi] and imbalance in the forces of yin and yang [negative and positive, respectively]. Practices such as herbs, meditation, massage, and acupuncture seek to aid healing by restoring the yin-yang balance and the flow of qi. . . . Ayurveda—a whole medical system that originated in India—. . . aims to integrate the body, mind, and spirit to prevent and treat disease. Therapies used include herbs, massage, and yoga.

Mind-Body Medicine

Mind-body medicine uses a variety of techniques designed to enhance the mind's capacity to affect bodily function and symptoms. Some techniques that were considered CAM in the past have become mainstream (for example, patient support groups and cognitive-behavioral therapy).

Other mind-body techniques are still considered CAM, including meditation—a conscious mental process using certain techniques, such as focusing attention or maintaining a specific posture, to suspend the stream of thoughts and relax the body and mind. [Other techniques that incorporate mind-body ideas include] prayer, mental healing, and therapies that use creative outlets such as art, music, or dance.

Biologically Based Practices

Biologically based practices in CAM use substances found in nature, such as herbs, foods, and vitamins. Some examples include dietary supplements, herbal products, and the use of other so-called natural but as yet scientifically unproven therapies (for example, using shark cartilage to treat cancer).

Manipulative and Body-Based Practices

Manipulative and body-based practices in CAM are based on manipulation, the application of controlled force to a joint, moving it beyond the normal range of motion in an effort to aid in restoring health. Manipulation may be performed as a part of other therapies or whole medical systems, including chiropractic medicine, massage, and naturopathy, and/or movement of one more parts of the body. Some examples include chiropractic or osteopathic manipulation—a type of manipulation practiced by osteopathic physicians. It is combined with physical therapy and instruction in proper posture, and [with] massage—pressing, rubbing, and moving muscles and other soft tissues of the body, primarily by using the hands and fingers. The aim is to increase the flow of blood and oxygen to the massaged area.

Energy Medicine

Energy therapies involve the use of energy fields. They are of two types:

Biofield therapies are intended to affect energy fields that purportedly surround and penetrate the human body. The existence of such fields has not yet been scientifically proven. Some forms of energy therapy manipulate biofields by applying pressure and/or manipulating the body by placing the hands in, or through, these fields.

Examples include qi gong—a component of traditional Chinese medicine that combines movement, meditation, and controlled breathing. The intent is to improve blood flow and the flow of qi. Reiki—a therapy in which practitioners seek to transmit a universal energy to a person, either from a distance or by placing their hands on or near that person—. . . [aims] to heal the spirit and thus the body. . . . Therapeutic Touch—a therapy in which practitioners pass their hands over another person's body—. . . [uses peoples'] own perceived . . . healing energy to identify energy imbalances and promote health.

Bioelectromagnetic-based therapies involve the unconventional use of electromagnetic fields, such as pulsed fields, magnetic fields, or alternating-current or direct-current fields.

Chiropractic Therapy Manually Adjusts the Musculoskeletal System to Promote Healing

National Women's Health Resource Center

National Women's Health Resource Center is a nonprofit health information source that develops and distributes women's health information based on the latest advances in medical research and practice.

The term "chiropractic" is derived from the Greek language and means "done by hand." Chiropractic therapy involves manual manipulation (primarily of the spine but can and often does include other manipulation of the musculoskeletal system (MSS) such as ankles, knees, hips, wrists, elbows, shoulders and ribs) to correct musculoskeletal disorders and improve overall health.

The Nature of Chiropractic Therapy

Chiropractic therapy is based on the theory that illness stems from blockages within spinal nerve roots, which exit the spine at regular intervals along its length. Chiropractors do not treat your illness unless the problem is directly musculoskeletally related. Instead, they seek to correct the MSS-related cause. If that problem is fixed, chiropractors say, the human body often has the ability to heal itself. So, chiropractors stress the importance of the relationship between the musculoskeletal system and the nervous system in regaining and sustaining health. They use adjustments, joint manipulation and other techniques to normalize spinal function, relieve various disorders and promote your body's natural healing process.

National Women's Health Resource Center, "Chiropractic Overview," healthywomen.org, December 15, 2005. http://www.healthywomen.org/healthtopics/chiropractic.

Chiropractors take a holistic approach to health, meaning they treat you and your body as a complete system. When one part or system is disabled, chiropractors believe it affects the entire system. They pay particular attention to preventive treatments to keep you well, such as changes in nutrition and exercise. The practice involves neither drugs nor surgery, but most chiropractors will advise you to consult with another health care professional if your condition requires a different type of treatment.

Spinal manipulation has been practiced for thousands of years.

Chiropractic is the most popular form of alternative health care in the U.S., according to a survey reported by the American Medical Association (AMA). The percentage of the population seeking chiropractic care ranges from 3.3 percent to 16 percent. Up to 100 million Americans have used chiropractic care, including 27 million in 1999 alone. The practice is licensed in every state and the District of Columbia, and there are at least 55,000 chiropractors in the U.S.

Spinal manipulation has been practiced for thousands of years, and modern chiropractic care is more than a century old. Modern chiropractic was initially established by Daniel David Palmer, who was seeking a way to cure disease without using drugs. Palmer concluded that most disease results from spinal misalignment and that many ailments are caused by the vertebrae impinging on spinal nerves. This impingement or blockage, he said at the turn of the 19th century, interferes with natural nerve transmission. He termed this condition "subluxation." Subluxation, he said, should be treated with manipulations or adjustments to properly align the spine and eliminate the blockage, restoring nerve transmission and allowing the body to heal itself. Dr. Palmer, however, was open to new scientific findings, something that was unusual at the turn of the 19th century.

Different Approaches

Today, there are several types of chiropractors, but most can be grouped into one of two basic schools. "Straight" chiropractors are purists, adhering to the philosophy that subluxations are responsible for most diseases. An element of this group spurns diagnosis and works to adhere to the early teachings of chiropractic. The much larger group—historically called "mixers"—uses various approaches and isn't limited to manipulation and adjustments. They perform diagnosis to the level of the general medical practitioner in order to work more closely with physicians. Like straight chiropractors, many mixers believe that certain disease processes are attributable to subluxations: others disagree. These differences of opinion are fading, and according to a report by the U.S. Agency for Health Care Policy and Research, more than two-thirds of chiropractors use techniques other than manipulation (such as exercise, nutritional counseling and physiotherapy), but 93 percent of the conditions treated by chiropractors are musculoskeletal in nature.

The larger group generally promote chiropractors as primary health care providers and are members of the American Chiropractic Association (ACA), the largest professional association for chiropractors.

There's a third, much smaller group of practitioners—many represented by the National Association for Chiropractic Medicine (NACM). It doesn't publish either its numbers or the names of its members, preferring to remain secretive while it cooperates with individuals and groups that are hostile to the chiropractic profession. This group focuses only on musculoskeletal back disorders. They do not treat other conditions, limiting their practice to spinal manipulative therapy.

NACM membership requirements state that a Doctor of Chiropractic Medicine must renounce the chiropractic hypothesis and/or philosophy: that is, that subluxation is the cause of disease. The chasm between the American Chiropractic Association—the largest and more progressive of the chiropractic groups—and the other groups is wide and contentious.

Applications of Chiropractic Care

Some chiropractors limit their practices to back pain, headache and similar musculoskeletal complaints, but some contend that chiropractic manipulation is the appropriate treatment for a wide-range of conditions, including those that aren't related to the musculoskeletal system. Most also focus on preventive care, which may include regular adjustments of returning musculoskeletal imbalances for health maintenance.

Studies indicate that chiropractic patients are more satisfied with their treatment than are those who receive traditional medical care.

Many health care professionals (including many chiropractors) contend that chiropractic treatment should focus only on musculoskeletal conditions. And, in fact, studies show that chiropractic manipulation seems to have the best results for acute back pain, particularly lower-back pain. It may also be an effective therapy for muscle spasms, nerve inflammation, headache, joint pain and various other musculoskeletal problems. According to a RAND [a public policy organization] study, more than 94 percent of all spinal manipulations are administered by chiropractors.

Many chiropractors also address problems unique to women, suggesting chiropractic care for pregnant and postpartum women, as well as those suffering from premenstrual syndrome and menstrual cramps. According to a study performed through the National University of Health Sciences, 88 percent of women receiving chiropractic treatment said it reduced menstrual pain. *The Journal of Manipulative and Physiological Therapeutics* reported that spinal manipulation might provide short-term relief of menstrual pain.

Chiropractic neurologists are a growing specialty, treating patients with a variety of conditions, including hyperactivity, attention deficit disorder and autism.

Sciatica (pain in the lower back and hip that spreads down the back of the thigh into the leg), asthma, high blood pressure, tension headaches, carpal tunnel syndrome, osteoporosis, severe temporomandibular joint dysfunction (TMD) and neurological pain are among the disorders treated by chiropractors, certain of them directly such as tension headaches, and others indirectly, such as osteoporosis, by addressing the symptoms. However, conditions of the blood, heart, lungs and other organs, as well as infectious diseases or injuries, require treatment by medical health care professionals. If you are under the care of a specialist, discuss your interest in chiropractic treatment with your health care team: don't ignore your regular course of treatment: many conditions today are more effectively co-managed by a variety of health care professionals.

Medical and chiropractic physicians have been in the process for many years now of building professional bridges. . . . [There should be] no difficulty attaining cooperation between a medical and a chiropractic doctor.

Increasing Acceptance

Chiropractic care has been the object of skepticism and even scorn by certain conventional health care professionals. But the practice has gained much respect in recent years, and many health care professionals will refer patients to chiropractors on occasion. A recent report from Washington state points out that fully 57 percent of medical doctors refer their patients with back pain to chiropractors and that two-thirds of them would like to learn more about exactly what it is chiropractors do. [Some] health plan[s] may even cover chiropractic treatment. Ninety-two percent of preferred provider organizations (PPOs) and 57 percent of health maintenance organizations (HMOs) include chiropractic benefits.

Active duty personnel in the U.S. armed forces now have guaranteed access to a permanent chiropractic benefit. On October 30, 2000, President Bill Clinton signed into law the National Defense Authorization Act for Fiscal Year 2001, requiring access to chiropractic services which includes, at a minimum, care for neuromusculoskeletal conditions typical among military personnel on active duty. The law requires that full implementation of the benefit be phased in over a five-year period, throughout all three service branches of the military. When completed, all active duty personnel stationed in the U.S. and overseas are to have access to chiropractic care.

A similar bill was signed into law in 2002, providing chiropractic care for United States Armed Forces veterans. It should be noted that 20 percent of all medical military discharges are for low back pain.

Respect for chiropractic has increased because of the therapy's track record as an appropriate treatment, particularly for early-stage lower-back pain, which is the second most costly medical problem in America. The *Journal of the American Medical Association* reported that chiropractic manipulation has been shown to have a "reasonably good degree of efficacy in relieving back pain, headaches and similar musculoskeletal problems."

Several studies indicate that chiropractic patients are more satisfied with their treatment than are those who receive traditional medical care and that they are less likely to seek care elsewhere for the same problem. Chiropractic patients also have the perception that chiropractors spend more face-to-face time with them than do their other health care professionals.

Acupuncture Overview

University of Maryland Medical Center

The University of Maryland Medical Center, part of the University of Maryland, is a hospital that provides comprehensive care for the Baltimore community and tertiary care for Maryland and the surrounding area.

Acupuncture is a treatment based on Traditional Chinese Medicine (TCM), a system of healing that dates back thousands of years. At the core of TCM is the notion that a type of life force, or energy, known as qi (pronounced "chee") flows through energy pathways (meridians) in the body. Each meridian corresponds to one organ, or group of organs, that governs particular bodily functions. Achieving the proper flow of qi is thought to create health and wellness. Qi maintains the dynamic balance of yin and yang, which are complementary opposites. According to TCM, everything in nature has both yin and yang. An imbalance of qi (too much, too little, or blocked flow) causes disease. To restore balance to the qi, an acupuncturist inserts needles at points along the meridians. These acupuncture points are places where the energy pathway is close to the surface of the skin.

What Is the History of Acupuncture?

The earliest recorded use of acupuncture dates from 200 BCE. Knowledge of acupuncture spread from China along Arab trade routes towards the West. However, up until the early 1970s, most Americans had never heard of acupuncture.

Acupuncture gained attention in the United States when President Nixon visited China in 1972. Traveling with Nixon was *New York Times* reporter James Reston, who received acu-

University of Maryland Medical Center, "Acupuncture Overview," September 17, 2005. www.umm.edu/altmed/articles/acupuncture-000345.htm.

puncture in China after undergoing an emergency appendectomy. Reston was so impressed with the post-operative pain relief he experienced from the procedure that he wrote about acupuncture upon returning to the United States.

A study using images of the brain confirmed that acupuncture increases our pain threshold, which may explain why it produces long-term pain relief.

In 1997, the U.S. National Institutes of Health formally recognized acupuncture as a mainstream medicine healing option with a statement documenting the procedure's safety and efficacy for treating a range of health conditions. While awareness of acupuncture is growing, many conventional physicians are still unfamiliar with both the theory and practice of acupuncture.

How Does Acupuncture Work?

The effects of acupuncture are complex. How it works is not entirely clear. Research suggests that the needling process, and other techniques used in acupuncture, may produce a variety of effects in the body and the brain. One theory is that stimulated nerve fibers transmit signals to the spinal cord and brain activating the body's central nervous system. The spinal cord and brain then release hormones responsible for making us feel less pain while improving overall health. In fact, a study using images of the brain confirmed that acupuncture increases our pain threshold, which may explain why it produces long-term pain relief. Acupuncture may also increase blood circulation and body temperature, affect white blood cell activity (responsible for our immune function), reduce cholesterol and triglyceride levels, and regulate blood sugar levels.

What Does an Acupuncturist Do?

In addition to asking questions, the acupuncturist may want to take your pulse at several points along the wrist and look at the shape, color, and coating of your tongue. The acupuncturist may also look at the color and texture of your skin, your posture, and other physical characteristics that offer clues to your health. You will lie down on a padded examining table, and the acupuncturist will insert the needles, twirling or gently jiggling each as it goes in. You may not feel the needles at all, or you may feel a twitch or a quick twinge of pain that disappears when the needle is completely inserted. Once the needles are all in place, you rest for 15 to 60 minutes. During this time, you'll probably feel relaxed and sleepy and may even doze off. At the end of the session, the acupuncturist quickly and painlessly removes the needles.

For certain conditions, acupuncture is more effective when the needles are heated using a technique known as "moxibustion." The acupuncturist lights a small bunch of the dried herb moxa (mugwort) and holds it above the needles. The herb, which burns slowly and gives off a little smoke and a pleasant, incense-like smell, never touches the body. Another variation is electrical acupuncture. This technique consists of hooking up electrical wires to the needles and running a weak current through them. In this procedure, you may feel a mild tingling, or nothing at all. Acupuncturists trained in Chinese herbal preparations may prescribe herbs along with acupuncture.

Are There Different Styles of Acupuncture?

There are several different approaches to acupuncture. Among the most common in the United States today are:

- TCM-based acupuncture—the most commonly practiced in the United States, it bases a diagnosis on eight principles of complementary opposites (yin/yang, internal/external, excess/deficiency, hot/cold).

- French energetic acupuncture—mostly used by MD acupuncturists, it emphasizes meridian patterns, in particular the yin-yang pairs of primary meridians.
- Korean hand acupuncture—based on the principle that the hands and feet have concentrations of qi, and that applying acupuncture needles to these areas is effective for the entire body.
- Auricular acupuncture—this technique is widely used in treating addiction disorders. It is based on the idea that the ear is a reflection of the body and that applying acupuncture needles to certain points on the ear affects corresponding organs.
- Myofascially-based acupuncture—often practiced by physical therapists, it involves feeling the meridian lines in search of tender points, then applying needles. Tender points indicate areas of abnormal energy flow.
- Japanese styles of acupuncture—sometimes referred to as "meridian therapy," it emphasizes needling technique and feeling meridians in diagnosis.

Both the World Health Organization and the National Institutes of Health recognize that acupuncture can be a helpful part of a treatment plan for many illnesses.

How Many Treatments Do I Need?

The number of acupuncture treatments you need depends on the complexity of your illness, whether it's a chronic or recent condition, and your general health. For example, you may need only one treatment for a recent wrist sprain, while a long-standing, chronic illness may require treatments once or twice a week for several months to achieve good results.

What Is Acupuncture Good For?

Acupuncture is particularly effective for pain relief and for post-surgery and chemotherapy-associated nausea and vomiting. In addition, both the World Health Organization and the National Institutes of Health recognize that acupuncture can be a helpful part of a treatment plan for many illnesses. A partial list includes: addiction (such as alcoholism), asthma, bronchitis, carpal tunnel syndrome, constipation, diarrhea, facial tics, fibromyalgia, headaches, irregular periods, low back pain, menopausal symptoms, menstrual cramps, osteoarthritis, sinusitis, spastic colon (often called irritable bowel syndrome), stroke rehabilitation, tendinitis, tennis elbow, and urinary problems such as incontinence. You can safely combine acupuncture with prescription drugs and other conventional treatments, but it is important for your primary care physician to be aware of and monitor how your acupuncture treatment may be affecting your conventional therapies.

The American Academy of Medical Acupuncture also lists a wide range of conditions for which acupuncture is appropriate. In addition to those listed above, they recommend acupuncture for sports injuries, sprains, strains, whiplash, neck pain, sciatica, nerve pain due to compression, overuse syndromes similar to carpal tunnel syndrome, pain resulting from spinal cord injuries, allergies, tinnitus (ringing in the ears), sore throat (called pharyngitis), high blood pressure, gastroesophageal reflux (felt as heartburn or indigestion), ulcers, chronic and recurrent bladder and kidney infections, premenstrual syndrome (PMS), infertility, endometriosis, memory problems, insomnia, multiple sclerosis, sensory disturbances, depression, anxiety, and other psychological disorders.

Should Anyone Avoid Acupuncture?

Some physicians and practitioners may avoid treatment during pregnancy. However, if you were seeing a practitioner prior to your pregnancy it is generally safe to continue receiving treatment from them during your pregnancy. You should inform your acupuncturist about any treatments or medications you are taking and all medical conditions you have. Acupuncture is not recommended during the menstrual cycle.

Should I Watch Out for Anything?

Be sure your acupuncturist uses only disposable needles. If your acupuncturist prescribes herbs and would like you to take them as part of your treatment, discuss this with your physician. Herbs are potent substances that can be harmful if you suffer from certain conditions. They can also interact with drugs you may be taking and cause side effects. Avoid strenuous physical activity, heavy meals, alcohol intake, or sexual activity for up to 8 hours after a treatment.

How Can I Find a Qualified Practitioner?

Most states require acupuncturists to be licensed and confer a title (LAc). The American Academy of Medical Acupuncture can provide a list of licensed physicians in your area who are also trained to perform acupuncture. The National Certification Commission for Acupuncture and Oriental Medicine certifies acupuncturists (Dipl Ac) and practitioners of Chinese herbal medicine (Dipl CH) upon passing a qualifying exam.

Does My Medical Insurance Cover Acupuncture Treatments?

An increasing number of insurance providers and HMOs [health maintenance organizations] cover all or part of the cost of acupuncture treatments, but these providers may have restrictions on the types of illnesses they cover. Check with your insurance company to see what your policy offers.

Massage Therapy Seeks to Relieve Stress and Muscle/Joint Pain

Cathy Wong

Cathy Wong is a licensed naturopathic doctor and certified nutrition specialist with the American College of Nutrition who writes frequently about complementary and alternative medicine.

Massage therapy, also known as Swedish massage, is the most common form of massage therapy in the United States. Massage therapists use long, smooth strokes, kneading and other movements focused on superficial layers of muscle using massage oil or lotion.

Massage therapy improves circulation by bringing oxygen and other nutrients to body tissues. It relieves muscle tension and pain, increases flexibility and mobility, and helps clear lactic acid and other waste, which reduces pain and stiffness in muscles and joints.

People get massage therapy for relaxation or for a variety of health conditions:

- Back pain
- Inflammatory conditions such as arthritis and tendinitis
- Stress relief and stress-related conditions
- Headaches and migraines
- Muscle and related conditions such as spasms, strains and sprains

Cathy Wong, "Massage Therapy," *About.com*, October 25, 2007. http://altmedicine.about.com/od/treatmentsmtoq/a/massage.htm.

- Repetitive strain injury, such as carpal tunnel syndrome
- Circulatory and respiratory problems
- Post-injury and post-surgical rehabilitation

A typical massage therapy session is between 40 and 90 minutes.

Massage therapy relieves stress. It is thought to help the body's stress response by lowering levels of hormones such as cortisol. Massage therapy also appears to enhance immune function.

A typical massage therapy session is between 40 and 90 minutes. The massage will begin with a brief consultation and review of symptoms, medical history, and lifestyle. The client is asked to undress (many people keep their underwear on) while the massage therapist is out of the room, and lies face down under a sheet on a padded massage table. The massage therapist will knock on the door to make sure the client is ready. The massage therapist re-enters the room and will then adjust the face rest and pillows to ensure that the client is comfortable and properly positioned. . . .

The massage therapist uses a light oil or lotion on the skin and begins the massage. A full body massage usually begins on the back and then moves down to the legs. The client will then be asked to turn over so they are face up. The massage continues on the client's arms, legs, neck, and abdomen. The client is underneath the sheet at all times, and in North America, only the part of the body being treated at any one time is uncovered.

After the massage, the massage therapist leaves the room so the client can get changed. . . .

Massage therapy shouldn't hurt. Occasionally there is mild aching when the massage therapist applies pressure over "knots" and other areas of muscle tension. . . .

Most people feel calm and relaxed after a treatment. Occasionally, people experience mild temporary aching for a day.

Precautions

Massage therapy is not recommended for certain people:

- People with infectious skin disease, rash, or open wounds
- Immediately after surgery
- Immediately after chemotherapy or radiation, unless recommended by your doctor
- People prone to blood clots. There is a risk of blood clots being dislodged. If you have heart disease, check with your doctor before having a massage
- Pregnant women should check with their doctor first if they are considering getting a massage. Massage in pregnant women should be done by massage therapists who are certified in pregnancy massage.

Massage should not be done directly over bruises, inflamed skin, unhealed wounds, tumors, abdominal hernia, or areas of recent fractures. [In addition,] . . . don't eat a heavy meal before the massage. [And] if it's your first time at the clinic or spa, arrive at least 10 minutes early to complete the necessary forms. Otherwise, arrive 5 minutes early so you can have a few minutes to rest and relax before starting the massage.

Homeopathy Treats Symptoms with Like Substances

Psychology Today

Psychology Today *is a U.S.-based magazine that deals with issues of emotional well-being, family and human relationships, and other matters related to psychology and mental health.*

Homeopathy is a form of medicine that treats illness through the administration of highly diluted herbs, animal substances, and chemical compounds.

The premise of homeopathy is that illnesses can be cured through the use of tiny doses of substances that would normally produce symptoms analogous to those being treated. Hence the term homeopathy: the word comes from the Greek *homeo* meaning "similar," and *pathos* meaning "suffering." A substance that would typically produce the symptoms of the illness under treatment is believed to stimulate healing. The substance in onions that causes watering eyes and runny noses, for instance, could be used to treat allergies. Malaria, whose symptoms include anxiety, dehydration, aches, and chills, can be treated with cinchona, a South American tree bark that produces identical symptoms. Samuel Hahnemann, the German doctor who developed homeopathy in the late 18th century, called this principle—which he described as treating like with like—the Law of Similarities.

A Controversial Therapy

Homeopathy has been controversial from its outset. Homeopaths view symptoms as the body's natural reaction to fighting an illness, whereas conventional medicine considers symptoms to be part of the illness and aims to suppress them.

Even more contentious is Hahnemann's Law of Potentization—the idea that homeopathic medicines grow stronger as they become more dilute. It contradicts basic laws of chemistry. Homeopathy is premised on a process called serial dilution, in which a drug is added to water or alcohol, then shaken, then diluted with more water or alcohol, then shaken, and so on. Homeopaths believe that the shaking at each stage of the dilution, called potentization, removes negative side effects of the substance while retaining its curative properties. The process results in solutions so dilute—typically around one part remedy to one-quadrillion parts water—that not a single molecule of the original substance remains in any given dose. Homeopaths believe that the "memory" of the substance remains, and that this "imprint" produces a therapeutic effect. Critics contend that any healing resulting from homeopathic treatment is merely a placebo effect.

In 1991, Dutch epidemiologists analyzed 105 studies of homeopathic treatment from 1966 to 1990. Eighty-one studies found patients had benefited from homeopathy, prompting the conclusion that "the evidence is to a large extent positive. It would probably be sufficient for establishing homeopathy as a treatment for certain conditions."

Is Homeopathy Right for You?

From acne to yellow fever, most health issues that can be addressed by your general practitioner can be successfully treated homeopathically. Homeopathy is appealing to many people because it is natural and safe, has no harsh side effects, and is administered in a positive, happy atmosphere by a caring practitioner who is trained to take the time to listen to you and discuss your health issues—as opposed to the sterility and anonymity that accompany much of conventional medicine. Just as important, homeopathy treats the entire person, mental, emotional, and physical, not just the narrowest physically defined medical problem. Many people like the simplicity of homeopathy—no matter how many symptoms you're experiencing, you'll take only one remedy, and that remedy will be aimed at all your symptoms. Finally, many people consider homeopathy when they have a recurring health issue that does not respond to conventional medicine.

Homeopathic remedies speed recovery by stimulating the vital force.

Homeopaths believe that illness is often the result of a disruption of the body's vital force—the energy necessary to maintain a healthy body and defend against disease. Treatment therefore addresses disruptions in one's vital force—those that may have resulted from stress, poor diet, lack of exercise, or environmental changes. Conventional medicine sometimes refers to this energy as the body's own healing power.

Homeopathic remedies speed recovery by stimulating the vital force. The most effective remedies match the symptom profile as accurately as possible, while also taking into account diet, exercise habits, lifestyle, and family medical history. A homeopath tries to identify a patient's constitutional type, which will help point to one of the hundreds of frequently used preventive and curative remedies. For example, someone with a "phosphorus constitution" may be prone to anxiety, circulatory problems, and digestive disorders, and will respond to the "phosphorus remedy," regardless of the specific illness.

Find a homeopath you feel comfortable working with, so that you can agree on a treatment plan that works for both of you. Also make sure that the person you select has experience treating your specific ailments and understands your specific needs.

Homeopathic Training

Although homeopathy is part of the field of alternative medicine, a medical degree is not needed to practice it. Physicians, physician assistants, nurse practitioners, nurses, naturopaths, chiropractors, and acupuncturists have access to a variety of training programs in homeopathy. The training programs vary in sophistication from weekend workshops to four-year courses. Homeopathic certifications include RSHom NA, Registered by the North American Society of Homeopaths; CCH, Certified by the Council for Homeopathic Certification; DHANP, Diplomate of the Homeopathic Academy of Naturopathic Physicians; DHt, Diplomate in Homeotherapeutics by the American Board of Homeotherapeutics.

As with any therapy, a personal connection with the practitioner can be as important as the technique itself, so choose a homeopath whom you can trust, one who readily addresses questions or concerns you have. Keep looking until you find someone who inspires confidence.

Dietary Supplements Seek to Promote Good Health

Walter C. Willet

Walter C. Willet is a physician and chairs the Department of Nutrition at the Harvard School of Public Health.

Once upon a time, vitamins were thought of only as nutrients needed in small amounts to prevent diseases with exotic-sounding names such as beriberi, pellagra, scurvy and rickets. Because these diseases were becoming rarer, it seemed that most Americans were getting enough vitamins.

New findings suggest that some people—probably many people—don't get enough of the essential micronutrients. Vitamins are playing newly recognized, or suspected, roles in preventing many diseases. By increasing the amount of vitamins and minerals we get, mostly from food, but maybe from supplements as well, we could substantially improve our long-term health.

The Three B's

The five vitamins that most people don't get enough of in their diets are folic acid, vitamin B6, vitamin B12, vitamin D and vitamin E. Three of these are B vitamins—B6, B12 and folic acid. There are a total of eight B vitamins, but new evidence suggests that these three may play pivotal roles in reducing heart disease and cancer.

High levels of the amino acid homocysteine are being studied as a risk factor for heart disease, and B6, B12 and folic acid help recycle homocysteine into harmless amino acids. The Physicians' Health Study, a long-term study of 22,000 men, found that high homocysteine levels tripled the chances of having a heart attack. The Nurses' Health Study, which recorded data from 121,000 female nurses, found that those with the highest intakes of vitamin B6 and folic acid were about half as likely to have heart attacks or die from heart disease as women with the lowest intakes.

Folic acid, or folate, also helps guide the development of the embryonic spinal cord. Pregnant women who get too little folic acid increase the chances that their babies will be born with neural tube defects such as spina bifida and anencephaly. Folic acid also may temper the increase in breast cancer seen in women who average more than one alcoholic drink per day. The same is true for colon cancer, another disease that is more common among alcohol drinkers than nondrinkers.

Getting enough of these vitamins doesn't mean taking megadoses. For most people, it means just reaching the current recommended daily intakes of 400 micrograms for folic acid, 1.3 to 1.7 milligrams for vitamin B6—depending on your age and gender—and 2.4 micrograms of vitamin B12. Good sources of B6 include meat, nuts and beans. Liver is the most efficient food source of B12 and is rich in folic acid. Unfortunately, only a small fraction of U.S. adults achieve the recommended levels of these B vitamins through diet alone.

Vitamin D

Vitamin D is a hormone made by your skin. Most of what we get from food comes from dairy products (which, by law, must be fortified with vitamin D), vitamin-fortified breakfast cereals and eggs from hens fed vitamin D. Although calcium usually gets all the credit for building bones and preventing fractures, vitamin D should get at least equal billing.

There are other reasons for getting more vitamin D. In test tubes, vitamin D strongly inhibits the growth and reproduction of a variety of cancer cells, including those of the breast, ovary, colon, prostate and brain. New studies suggest that the same thing happens in our bodies. Several small studies suggest that getting more vitamin D, especially from sunlight, helps lower blood pressure. Getting too little may contribute to heart failure and peripheral artery disease (blocked blood flow in the legs) and may be implicated in the artery-clogging process known as atherosclerosis. In the Nurses' Health Study, women who took vitamin D supplements were about half as likely to develop multiple sclerosis as those who didn't.

A multivitamin can't in any way replace healthy eating.

People who can bask in strong sunlight for a few minutes on most days year-round make plenty of vitamin D, but that rules out everyone living north of San Francisco, Denver, Indianapolis and Philadelphia: During the winter months, the amount of ultraviolet light hitting those northern regions isn't enough to generate vitamin D. It also rules out people who can't get out for a 15-minute walk when the sun is high in the sky—in other words, millions of people. Your best bet is to find a multivitamin that delivers 800 to 1,000 International Units (IU) of vitamin D. A standard multivitamin plus a vitamin D supplement is another option.

Vitamin E

In the Nurses' Health Study and the Health Professionals Follow-up Study, we saw lower risks of heart disease in women and men who took vitamin E supplements of at least 100 IU for at least two years. At the end of 2004, an international team pooled the data from nine long-term studies in order to tease out whether vitamin E had an impact on heart disease. According to the researchers, "The results weakly support the hypothesis that higher dietary intake of vitamin E . . . reduces the risk of coronary heart disease." At the beginning of 2005, an analysis of the results of 19 vitamin E trials suggested that users of high-dose vitamin E (more than 400 IU per day) might have a slightly higher death rate than non-users. However, most of the trials in the analysis included only volunteers with heart disease, and an exhaustive review of vitamin E by the Institute of Medicine showed it is safe at much higher doses. In a recent large trial among women, vitamin E supplements reduced total cardiovascular deaths by 24 percent. The final role of vitamin E in preventing heart disease remains unsettled, but it is wise not to rely only on high doses of vitamin E to protect you against a heart attack or stroke.

Some early studies suggest that vitamin E supplements may prevent age-related dementia. Another promising line of research involves vitamin E and amyotrophic lateral sclerosis (Lou Gehrig's disease). Vitamin E can be found in many nuts, whole grains and leafy greens, but unlike many other vitamins, vitamin E is not present in food alone at levels thought to be protective—and at the levels used in most studies.

Getting 400 IU of vitamin E means taking a high-E multivitamin or a vitamin E supplement along with a typical multivitamin. Because vitamin E can reduce the blood's ability to clot, people who take blood thinners should talk with their health-care providers before taking vitamin E supplements.

Supplements: What to Look For

A multivitamin can't in any way replace healthy eating. It gives you barely a scintilla of the vast array of healthful nutrients found in food. But it does offer a nutritional backup to fill in the holes that can plague even the most conscientious eaters. Research is pointing ever more strongly to the fact that several ingredients in a standard multivitamin—especially vitamins B6 and B12, folic acid and vitamin D—are essential players in preventing heart disease, cancer, osteoporosis and other chronic diseases. A year's supply usually costs less than $40, or about a dime a day—it's the best nutritional bang for your buck.

You don't need a designer vitamin, a name-brand vitamin, or an "all-natural" formulation. A store-brand, RDA [recommended daily amount]-level multivitamin is a perfectly fine place to start. Avoid getting too much preformed vitamin A, also called retinol, which can block the effects of vitamin D. When shopping for a multivitamin, look for one that gets all or most of its vitamin A content from beta carotene. Try to keep your intake of retinol from supplements to less than 2,000 IU [international units] per day. Too much zinc also can be a problem. It's relatively easy to get too much zinc from supplements, and symptoms of zinc overload can begin appearing with just a little over 15 milligrams per day. These include a depressed immune system, poor wound healing and skin problems. High zinc intake also may promote the development or growth of prostate cancer. Despite the fact that most U.S. residents actually get less than the recommended daily amount of zinc, there's little evidence that these lower levels cause health problems.

There's no consensus on ideal vitamin intakes because scientific knowledge about them is still evolving.

Extra vitamin D is definitely worth pursuing. Standard multivitamins offer 400 IU, less than half of what's needed for optimal health. You can make up the other 400 to 600 IU by taking a separate vitamin D tablet or capsule. A few companies are making supplements that replace most of the preformed vitamin A with beta carotene and contain adequate doses of vitamin D. One example is the Basic One multivitamin formulated by Dr. Kenneth Cooper. It contains plenty of vitamin A (3,000 IU), all in the form of beta carotene and other carotenoids, along with 800 IU of vitamin D.

For most people without heart disease, an extra vitamin E supplement probably makes sense. Even though the ending to the vitamin E story hasn't yet been written, at least 400 milligrams a day may be needed for optimal health. Standard multivitamins contain only 30 IU.

So far, there's no consensus on ideal vitamin intakes because scientific knowledge about them is still evolving. We could definitely use more evidence about the benefits of commonly used vitamins. At the same time, harm isn't likely when they are taken in reasonable doses, and the cost is minimal. In this situation, it seems a bit foolish to demand that all the evidentiary "i's" be dotted and "t's" crossed before acting.

Energy Healers Work with the Body's Energy Field

National Center for Complementary and Alternative Medicine (NCCAM)

The National Center for Complementary and Alternative Medicine is the federal government's lead agency for scientific research on complementary and alternative medicine. It is one of the twenty-seven institutes and centers that make up the National Institutes of Health within the U.S. Department of Health and Human Services.

Energy medicine is a domain in CAM that deals with energy fields of two types:

- Veritable, which can be measured
- Putative, which have yet to be measured

The veritable energies employ mechanical vibrations (such as sound) and electromagnetic forces, including visible light, magnetism, monochromatic radiation (such as laser beams), and rays from other parts of the electromagnetic spectrum. They involve the use of specific, measurable wavelengths and frequencies to treat patients.

In contrast, putative energy fields (also called biofields) have defied measurement to date by reproducible methods. Therapies involving putative energy fields are based on the concept that human beings are infused with a subtle form of energy. This vital energy or life force is known under different names in different cultures, such as qi [chi] in traditional Chinese medicine (TCM), ki in the Japanese Kampo system, doshas in Ayurvedic medicine, and elsewhere as prana, etheric energy, fohat, orgone, odic force, mana, and homeopathic resonance. Vital energy is believed to flow throughout the ma-

National Center for Complementary and Alternative Medicine, "Energy Medicine: An Overview," March 2007. http://nccam.nih.gov/about/ataglance/

terial human body, but it has not been unequivocally measured by means of conventional instrumentation. Nonetheless, therapists claim that they can work with this subtle energy, see it with their own eyes, and use it to effect changes in the physical body and influence health.

Practices Involving Energy Fields

Practitioners of energy medicine believe that illness results from disturbances of these subtle energies (the biofield). For example, more than 2,000 years ago, Asian practitioners postulated that the flow and balance of life energies are necessary for maintaining health and described tools to restore them. Herbal medicine, acupuncture, acupressure, moxibustion, and cupping, for example, are all believed to act by correcting imbalances in the internal biofield, such as by restoring the flow of qi through meridians to reinstate health. Some therapists are believed to emit or transmit the vital energy (external qi) to a recipient to restore health.

Examples of practices involving putative energy fields include:

- Reiki and Johrei, both of Japanese origin
- Qi gong, a Chinese practice
- Healing touch, in which the therapist is purported to identify imbalances and correct a client's energy by passing his or her hands over the patient
- Intercessory prayer, in which a person intercedes through prayer on behalf of another

In the aggregate, these approaches are among the most controversial of CAM practices because neither the external energy fields nor their therapeutic effects have been demonstrated convincingly by any biophysical means. Yet, energy medicine is gaining popularity in the American marketplace and has become a subject of investigations at some academic medical centers. A recent National Center for Health Statistics survey indicated that approximately 1 percent of the participants had used Reiki, 0.5 percent had used qi gong, 4.6 percent had used some kind of healing ritual.

Veritable Energy Medicine

There are many well-established uses for the application of measurable energy fields to diagnose or treat diseases: electromagnetic fields in magnetic resonance imaging, cardiac pacemakers, radiation therapy, ultraviolet light for psoriasis, laser keratoplasty, and more. There are many other claimed uses as well. The ability to deliver quantifiable amounts of energies across the electromagnetic spectrum is an advantage to studies of their mechanisms and clinical effects. For example, both static and pulsating electromagnetic therapies have been employed.

Specific sound frequencies resonate with specific organs of the body to heal and support the body.

Static magnets have been used for centuries in efforts to relieve pain or to obtain other alleged benefits (e.g., increased energy). Numerous anecdotal reports have indicated that individuals have experienced significant, and at times dramatic, relief of pain after the application of static magnets over a painful area. Although the literature on the biological effects of magnetic fields is growing, there is a paucity of data from well-structured, clinically sound studies. However, there is growing evidence that magnetic fields can influence physiological processes. It has recently been shown that static magnetic fields affect the microvasculature of skeletal muscle. Microvessels that are initially dilated respond to a magnetic field by constricting, and microvessels that are initially constricted respond by dilating. These results suggest that static magnetic fields may have a beneficial role in treating edema or ischemic conditions, but there is no proof that they do.

Pulsating electromagnetic therapy has been in use for the past 40 years. A well-recognized and standard use is to enhance the healing of nonunion fractures. It also has been claimed that this therapy is effective in treating osteoarthritis, migraine headaches, multiple sclerosis, and sleep disorders. Some animal and cell culture studies have been conducted to elucidate the basic mechanism of the pulsating electromagnetic therapy effect, such as cell proliferation and cell-surface binding for growth factors. However, detailed data on the mechanisms of action are still lacking.

Low-power millimeter wave (MW) irradiation elicits biological effects, and clinicians in Russia and other parts of Eastern Europe have used it in past decades to treat a variety of conditions, ranging from skin diseases and wound healing to various types of cancer, gastrointestinal and cardiovascular diseases, and psychiatric illnesses. In spite of an increasing number of *in vivo* and *in vitro* studies, the nature of MW action is not well understood. It has been shown, for example, that MW irradiation can augment T-cell mediated immunity in vitro. However, the mechanisms by which MW irradiation enhances T-cell functions are not known. Some studies indicate that pretreating mice with naloxone may block the hypoalgesic [pain-reducing] and antipruritic [itch-relieving] effects of MW irradiation, suggesting that endogenous opioids are involved in MW therapy-induced hypoalgesia. Theoretical and experimental data show that nearly all the MW energy is absorbed in the superficial layers of skin, but it is not clear how the energy absorbed by keratinocytes, the main constituents of epidermis, is transmitted to elicit the therapeutic effect. It is also unclear whether MW yields clinical effects beyond a placebo response.

Sound energy therapy, sometimes referred to as vibrational or frequency therapy, includes music therapy as well as wind chime and tuning fork therapy. The presumptive basis of its effect is that specific sound frequencies resonate with specific organs of the body to heal and support the body. Music therapy has been the most studied among these interventions, with studies dating back to the 1920s, when it was reported that music affected blood pressure. Other studies have suggested that music can help reduce pain and anxiety. Music and imagery, alone and in combination, have been used to entrain mood states, reduce acute or chronic pain, and alter certain biochemicals, such as plasma beta-endorphin levels. These uses of energy fields truly overlap with the domain of mind-body medicine.

The concept that sickness and disease arise from imbalances in the vital energy field of the body has led to many forms of therapy.

Light therapy is the use of natural or artificial light to treat various ailments, but unproven uses of light extend to lasers, colors, and monochromatic lights. High-intensity light therapy has been documented to be useful for seasonal affective disorder, with less evidence for its usefulness in the treatment of more general forms of depression and sleep disorders. Hormonal changes have been detected after treatment. Although low-level laser therapy is claimed to be useful for relieving pain, reducing inflammation, and helping to heal wounds, strong scientific proof of these effects is still needed.

Putative Energy Fields

The concept that sickness and disease arise from imbalances in the vital energy field of the body has led to many forms of therapy. In TCM, a series of approaches are taken to rectify the flow of qi, such as herbal medicine, acupuncture (and its various versions), qi gong, diet, and behavior changes.

Of these approaches, acupuncture is the most prominent therapy to promote qi flow along the meridians. Acupuncture has been extensively studied and has been shown to be effective in treating some conditions, particularly certain forms of pain. However, its mechanism of action remains to be elucidated. The main threads of research on acupuncture have shown regional effects on neurotransmitter expression, but have not validated the existence of an "energy" per se.

Qi gong, another energy modality that purportedly can restore health, is practiced widely in the clinics and hospitals of China. Most of the reports were published as abstracts in Chinese, which makes accessing the information difficult. But [researcher Kenneth] Sancier has collected more than 2,000 records in his qi gong database which indicates that qi gong has extensive health benefits on conditions ranging from blood pressure to asthma. The reported studies, however, are largely anecdotal case series and not randomized controlled trials. Few studies have been conducted outside China and reported in peer-reviewed journals in English. There have been no large clinical trials.

Although modalities such as acupuncture and qi gong have been studied separately, TCM uses combinations of treatments (e.g., herbs, acupuncture, and qi gong) in practice. Similarly, Ayurvedic medicine uses combinations of herbal medicine, yoga, meditation, and other approaches to restore vital energy, particularly at the chakra energy centers.

Homeopathy

One Western approach with implications for energy medicine is homeopathy. Homeopaths believe that their remedies mobilize the body's vital force to orchestrate coordinated healing responses throughout the organism. The body translates the information on the vital force into local physical changes that lead to recovery from acute and chronic diseases. Homeopaths use their assessment of the deficits in vital force to guide dose (potency) selection and treatment pace, and to judge the likely clinical course and prognosis. Homeopathic medicine is based on the principle of similars, and remedies are often prescribed in high dilutions. In most cases, the dilution may not contain any molecules of the original agents at all. As a consequence, homoeopathic remedies, at least when applied in high dilutions, cannot act by pharmacological means. Theories for a potential mechanism of action invoke the homeopathic solution, therefore, postulating that information is stored in the dilution process by physical means. Other than a study reported by the Benveniste laboratory and other smaller studies, this hypothesis has not been supported by scientific research. There have been numerous clinical studies of homeopathic approaches, but systematic reviews point out the overall poor quality and inconsistency of these studies.

Proponents of energy field therapies also claim that some of these therapies can act across long distances.

Numerous other practices have evolved over the years to promote or maintain the balance of vital energy fields in the body. Examples of these modalities include Therapeutic Touch, healing touch, Reiki, Johrei, vortex healing, and polarity therapy. All these modalities involve movement of the practitioner's hands over the patient's body to become attuned to the condition of the patient, with the idea that by so doing, the practitioner is able to strengthen and reorient the patient's energies.

Many small studies of Therapeutic Touch have suggested its effectiveness in a wide variety of conditions, including wound healing, osteoarthritis, migraine headaches, and anxiety in burn patients. In a recent meta-analysis of 11 controlled Therapeutic Touch studies, 7 controlled studies had positive outcomes, and 3 showed no effect; in one study, the control group healed faster than the Therapeutic Touch group. Similarly, Reiki and Johrei practitioners claim that the therapies boost the body's immune system, enhance the body's ability to heal itself, and are beneficial for a wide range of problems, such as stress-related conditions, allergies, heart conditions, high blood pressure, and chronic pain. However, there has been little rigorous scientific research. Overall, these therapies have impressive anecdotal evidence, but none has been proven scientifically to be effective.

Proponents of energy field therapies also claim that some of these therapies can act across long distances. For example, the long-distance effects of external qi gong have been studied in China and summarized in the book *Scientific Qigong Exploration*, which has been translated into English. The studies reported various healing cases and described the nature of qi as bidirectional, multifunctional, adaptable to targets, and capable of effects over long distances. But none of these claims has been independently verified. Another form of distant healing is intercessory prayer, in which a person prays for the healing of another person who is a great distance away, with or without that person's knowledge. Review of eight nonrandomized and nine randomized clinical trials published between 2000 and 2002 showed that the majority of the more rigorous trials do not support the hypothesis that distant intercessory prayer has specific therapeutic effects.

There has always been an interest in detecting and describing the physical properties of putative energy fields. Kirlian photography, aura imaging, and gas discharge visualization are approaches for which dramatic and unique differences before and after therapeutic energy attunements or treatments have been claimed. However, it is not clear what is being detected or photographed. Early results demonstrated that gamma radiation levels markedly decreased during therapy sessions in 100 percent of subjects and at every body site tested, regardless of which therapist performed the treatment. Recently replicated studies identified statistically significant decreases in gamma rays emitted from patients during alternative healing sessions with trained practitioners.

It has been hypothesized that the body's primary gamma emitter, potassium-40 (K40), represents a "self-regulation" of energy within the body and the surrounding electromagnetic field. The body's energy adjustment may result, in part, from the increased electromagnetic fields surrounding the hands of the healers. Furthermore, an extremely sensitive magnetometer called a superconducting quantum interference device (SQUID) has been claimed to measure large frequency-pulsing biomagnetic fields emanating from the hands of Therapeutic Touch practitioners during therapy. In one study, a simple magnetometer measured and quantified similar frequency-pulsing biomagnetic fields from the hands of meditators and practitioners of yoga and qi gong. These fields were 1,000 times greater than the strongest human biomagnetic field and were in the same frequency range as those being tested in medical research laboratories for use in speeding the healing process of certain biological tissues. This range is low energy and extremely low frequency, spanning from 2 Hz to 50 Hz. However, there are considerable technical problems in such research. For example, SQUID measurement must be conducted under a special shielded environment, and the connection between electromagnetic field increases and observed healing benefits reported in the current literature is missing.

Other studies of putative energies suggested that energy fields from one person can overlap and interact with energy fields of other people. For example, when individuals touch, one person's electrocardiographic signal is registered in the other person's electroencephalogram (EEG) and elsewhere on the other person's body. In addition, one individual's cardiac signal can be registered in another's EEG recording when two people sit quietly opposite one another.

Additional Theories

Thus far, electromagnetic energy has been demonstrated and postulated to be the energy between bioenergy healers and patients. However, the exact nature of this energy is not clear. Among the range of ideas emerging in this field is the theory of a Russian researcher who recently hypothesized that "torsion fields" exist and that they can be propagated through space at no less than 10^9 times the speed of light in vacuum; that they convey information without transmitting energy; and that they are not required to obey the superposition principle.

There are other extraordinary claims and observations recorded in the literature. For example, one report claimed that accomplished meditators were able to imprint their intentions on electrical devices (IIED), which when placed in a room for 3 months, would elicit these intentions, such as changes in pH and temperature, in the room even when the IIED was removed from the room. Another claim is that water will crystallize into different forms and appearances under the influence of written intentions or types of music.

For research, questions remain about which of the above theories and approaches can be and should be addressed using existing technologies, and how.

Naturopathic Medicine Helps the Body Heal Itself

Alternativemedicinechannel

Alternativemedicinechannel is a Web site developed and administered by alternative medicine practitioners that provides information on alternative treatments for a variety of health issues.

Naturopathic medicine is a system of medicine that uses natural therapeutics to maintain health and bring about cure. It is based on vitalism, a medical philosophy that views a person as a vital being consisting of a body, mind, and spirit, all constantly interacting with each other in ways that are not yet understood, not just a complex mass of chemical and physical reactions. Vitalists assert that illness is not directly caused by a pathogen (disease-causing organism, i.e., virus, bacterium), but is the result of the body's response to a pathogen and its attempt to defend and heal itself. Given the opportunity, the body has the ability to heal itself. A naturopathic doctor assists the body by increasing resistance to pathogens and aiding the healing process.

The term "naturopathy" was first used around 1895 to describe the growing number of doctors and healers who believed that treating the person and promoting health were more important than simply alleviating the symptoms of disease. In 1902 Benedict Lust, considered the father of naturopathy, wrote: "In a word, Naturopathy stands for the reconciling, harmonizing and unifying of nature, humanity and God." During World War II, natural healing was pushed to the background by the development of medical technology and the increased use of drugs such as penicillin and morphine. Then, in the late 1960s, natural medicine began regaining re-

Alternativemedicinechannel, "Naturopathic Medicine: Overview," December 4, 2007. www.alternativemedicinechannel.com/naturopathic/index.shtml.

spect. Today, naturopathic medicine continues to grow in popularity and acceptance as people continue to look for alternatives to drugs and surgery.

Naturopathic doctors treat most conditions.

What Conditions Do Naturopaths Treat?

Naturopathic doctors treat most conditions. Naturopathic medicine can be used alone or in conjunction with other alternative methods or conventional medicine to treat the following:

- Acute conditions such as headaches, sore throats, colds and flu, intestinal upsets, ear infections, contact dermatitis, urinary tract infections, and sprains and strains.
- Chronic illnesses such as migraine, autoimmune disease, cardiovascular disease, arthritis, cancer, and musculoskeletal pain.
- Mental and emotional problems such as stress, depression, anxiety, and Anger.
- Pregnancy and childbirth.

What Methods Do Naturopaths Use?

Naturopathic doctors use the following diagnostic and treatment modalities:

Nutritional medicine—In 420 BC, Hippocrates, the father of medicine, said, "Leave your drugs in the chemist's pot if you can cure the patient with food." Many of the chronic health problems that plague Americans today are the result of poor dietary and lifestyle choices. Illnesses such as diabetes, cardiovascular disease, hypertension, cancer, and gastrointestinal problems develop as a consequence of the food we choose. By changing our diet and adopting a healthy lifestyle, we can often change or reverse the course of an illness and restore health. Naturopathic doctors are trained in assessing nutritional status and recommending dietary changes and vitamin and mineral supplementation.

Botanical medicine—Botanical medicine (phytotherapy) has been used for thousands of years. Current scientific studies have validated the use of many plants as medicines. Today, 80% of the world's population uses plants to treat illness. Plants are used medicinally because they do not have high toxicity, accumulate in the body, or cause addiction or withdrawal symptoms. Herbs are used to enhance immune function; improve digestion; normalize bodily functions; destroy bacteria, viruses, and fungi; soothe irritated tissues; calm nerves; and relax muscles. Examples of botanical treatments are teas, poultices, and tinctures.

Hydrotherapy—Hydrotherapy, or water therapy, is the application of water to initiate cure. It is a safe and painless therapy that can be done at home for all types of injury and illness. Some common hydrotherapy treatments are hot foot bath, constitutional hydrotherapy, warming socks, and the castor oil pack.

Homeopathy—In the 18th century, Dr. Samuel Hahnemann discovered that substances that cause specific symptoms in large doses could cure those same symptoms in infinitesimal doses. For example, when a healthy individual is given quinine in large doses, it produces symptoms of malaria. Yet, when very small doses of quinine are given to an individual with malaria, it helps ease the symptoms. This is known as the Law of Similars. Homeopathic medicines, known as remedies, are produced from animals, plants, and minerals. The naturopathic doctor prescribes remedies based on an individual's unique symptoms or characteristics. This means that two people who have the flu may receive different remedies because their symptoms are different. It requires training and skill to determine the appropriate remedy. When the appropriate remedy (called the similimum) is given, it can produce powerful and effective results. Homeopathy is used to treat all forms of acute and chronic illness and injury and is safe for children, pregnant or lactating women, and the elderly.

Diagnostic radiology and other imaging techniques.

Physical medicine (i.e., ultrasound, microcurrent, manipulation).

Minor surgery.

Naturopathic obstetrics (requires additional training).

The emphasis [of naturopathy] is on building health rather than treating disease.

Principles of Naturopathic Medicine

Naturopathic medicine is based on six principles.

The Healing Power of Nature—The body has the inherent ability to heal itself. This healing process is intelligent and ordered. Naturopathic doctors support and assist the healing process by identifying and removing obstacles to cure and by using natural methods and medicines that work with, not against, the body's natural processes.

Identify and Treat the Cause—Every illness has a cause. Causes may occur on the physical, mental, emotional, or spiritual level. Symptoms are expressions of the body's attempt to heal, but are not the cause of illness. Naturopathic doctors are trained to find and remove the underlying cause of an illness rather than just eliminate or suppress symptoms.

First Do No Harm—Naturopathic doctors use methods and medicines that minimize the risk of harmful side effects. Methods designed to suppress symptoms but not remove the underlying cause may be harmful, and their use is avoided.

Doctor as Teacher—The original meaning of the word "doctor" is teacher. A principal objective of naturopathic medicine is to educate the patient and emphasize self-responsibility for health.

Treat the Whole Person—When treating an individual, all aspects of that person (physical, mental, emotional, and spiritual) are taken into account.

Prevention Is the Best Cure—Illness is often due to diet, habits, and lifestyle. Naturopathic doctors assess risk factors and susceptibility to disease and make appropriate recommendations to prevent illness or to prevent minor illness from developing into more serious or chronic disease. The emphasis is on building health rather than treating disease.

CHAPTER 2

Are Alternative Therapies Safe?

Chapter Overview

Bridget Butler

Bridget Butler is a writer for the Weekly Reader publication Current Health 2.

When Abraham Cherrix, a 16-year-old from Chincoteague, Va., was diagnosed with cancer in 2005, he underwent the standard course of treatment—chemotherapy (heavy doses of cancer-fighting drugs). The treatment seemed to work but left Abraham exhausted and frail. When the cancer returned, Abraham and his family rejected another round of chemotherapy in favor of an herbal treatment at a clinic in Mexico. The state of Virginia tried to force Abraham to undergo chemo, but [in] summer [2006] a judge ruled that Abraham could skip the treatment if he worked with a cancer specialist who would coordinate both the conventional and alternative sides of the treatment plan. (At the last update, Abraham's tumor had shrunk, and he was feeling much more energetic.)

Abraham's court battle highlighted the interest that many teens and their families have in complementary and alternative medicine (CAM). This term describes health care that is not considered to be part of "mainstream medicine." It encompasses many different kinds of health treatments, some that are used instead of conventional medical remedies (alternative) and some that can be used in addition to standard treatments (complementary). Many different kinds of CAM exist, from brand-new techniques to those that have been used in other cultures for thousands of years.

So what exactly qualifies? The National Center for Complementary and Alternative Medicine (NCCAM), in association with the National Institutes of Health, groups CAM into five areas:

Bridget Butler, "A Different Path to Health," *Current Health 2*, vol. 33, January 2007.

1. complete systems of beliefs and practices, such as traditional Chinese medicine and naturopathic medicine, that rely on natural treatments to help the body heal itself;
2. natural treatments, relying on specific foods, vitamins, or herbs—remedies that use materials found in nature for their presumed health benefits;
3. healing techniques, such as Reiki or qigong, that use energy fields—either electromagnetic fields or those that allegedly surround the human body;
4. manipulative therapies, such as massage or chiropractic care, that involve moving or manipulating various body parts;
5. the mind-body connection, especially the mind's power to affect the body, including meditation, prayer, music therapy, and yoga.

There are other terms for CAM therapies, such as natural medicine, holistic health care, and mind/body/spirit medicine. No matter what they're called, these healing techniques have much in common. They emphasize the importance of preventing illness and of creating a sense of balance in the body. Most alternative therapies also emphasize a partnership between the patient and the caregiver that differs from the traditional doctor-patient relationship. An alternative-medicine practitioner often acts more like a mentor to the patient, helping the body heal itself.

[Some people] turn to CAM because it fits with their views about health; they feel that CAM focuses on staying healthy instead of just treating symptoms of sickness.

In the United States, CAM seems to be gaining in popularity, especially among teens. About 36 percent of Americans use some form of CAM, according to the NCCAM. That percentage increases to 62 when megavitamins and health-specific prayers are included. And in a survey conducted by researchers at the College of St. Benedict in St. Joseph, Minn., 68 percent of teens reported using one or more forms of CAM. Of those teens, 66 percent said their main reason for trying alternative treatments was to relieve aches and pains.

Some people turn to alternative medicine because they think the therapies have fewer side effects than prescription drugs do. Others turn to CAM because it fits with their views about health; they feel that CAM focuses on staying healthy instead of just treating symptoms of sickness. "Alternative doctors work with their patients to keep them strong and help them use their own natural strengths so that they don't get sick," says C. Evers Whyte, a chiropractor (someone who is trained to adjust the spine for better health) in Riverside, Conn.

If conventional medicine isn't helping with a health problem, "alternative medicine can usually be safely pursued," according to Jim Sullivan, an osteopath in York, Pa. (An osteopath is a medical doctor who evaluates and treats the whole person, not just isolated symptoms.)

Effectiveness of CAM

Is CAM any better than your usual doc's treatment? That all depends on whom you ask. Your dad might think taking herbal supplements is hogwash, but your neighbor swears they work for her. And 26 percent of people who use CAM try it on the advice of a conventional health-care provider, according to the NCCAM.

Scientific research on CAM is relatively new, but some studies have tested whether various alternative remedies are effective. For example, one 2004 study showed that acupuncture provided pain relief for people who suffered from osteoarthritis of the knee. But another study, published in 2005 in the *New England Journal of Medicine*, reported that an herbal remedy, echinacea, did not help prevent the common cold—although some critics felt the dose of the herb used in the study was too low.

Before using alternative remedies, check with your parents, your family doctor, or a licensed and respected natural health-care provider to make sure the remedy is OK to use.

Should you use CAM? It's important to always obtain an accurate diagnosis and to seek the most effective treatment available. For example, if you develop appendicitis, all the music therapy in the world won't heal it; that's a job for a surgeon. Likewise, prescription painkillers might not solve your chronic stomachaches if the cause is anxiety or depression. You might talk to your doctor about alternative treatment options if regular medical therapies aren't working for you. It's all about finding the treatment that works best to help you feel happy and healthy.

Safety of Alternative Medicine

Before using alternative remedies, check with your parents, your family doctor, or a licensed and respected natural health-care provider to make sure the remedy is OK to use. A bottle of supplements labeled "natural" may not be safe for you to take. Substances can interact with drugs, other supplements, or foods, and they may not even contain the substance listed on the label. (The U.S. Food and Drug Administration monitors medications but not vitamins or supplements.) Also make sure any alternative health-care provider you visit has the proper training, qualifications, and certifications to practice.

You just heard about a nonmedical treatment that you think will help with a health problem. How do you know whether it's for real or forgettable? Do your homework, according to the National Center for Complementary and Alternative Medicine (NCCAM).

- Search for real proof the treatment works. If an advertisement displays only personal testimonials, ask the manufacturer or practitioner for hard data. Be cautious if you don't get solid answers.
- See what trustworthy government sources, such as the NCCAM, the Food and Drug Administration, and the Federal Trade Commission (a consumer watchdog), have to say about it.
- Carefully read through the marketing language, and think about what it says—and doesn't say. If something sounds too good to be true, it probably is.

Popular Alternative Therapies

Here's a rundown of some popular CAM options tried by teens.

Remedy	What It Is	Helps With
Acupuncture	Acupuncture is a form of traditional Chinese medicine. Acupuncturists use thin needles on specific points on the body to balance the body's energy.	Managing pain and nausea, increasing circulation, and improving immune functions
Chiropractic Care	Chiropractors adjust joints, mostly in the spine, so they are aligned properly. Chiropractors may also work on muscles or recommend strengthening exercises.	Treating neck and back pain, sports injuries, and certain types of headaches

Remedy	What It Is	Helps With
Dietary Supplements	People ingest dietary supplements to add to the foods they eat. Supplements can contain substances such as vitamins, minerals, herbs, enzymes, and amino acids. Supplemental products also come in many forms: powders, liquids, tablets, and capsules.	Supplementing the diet. For example, someone who is allergic to dairy products might take a calcium supplement to make sure he or she gets enough calcium.
Massage Therapy	Massage is a healing technique in which structured pressure is applied to the body.	Relieving sore muscles, decreasing stress, improving circulation, healing an injury, and managing pain

Personal Accounts

Remedy	Teens Say
Acupuncture	"I really like it a lot. I usually go once a week and see a lot of improvement with pain. It doesn't hurt at all. It helps me relax and eases everything."—Helena Landegger, 16
Chiropractic Care	"I went to a chiropractor because I had pain in my shoulder. The adjustments not only helped my shoulder [but] also gave me more energy, decreased my anxiety, and improved my overall health. They even improved my posture."—Trevor Eddy, 18
Dietary Supplements	"I take chewable multivitamins. They taste pretty disgusting, but I take them because I think they're good for me."—Caty Cleskewicz, 14
Massage Therapy	"I strained a muscle in my calf while running, so before track and cross-country practice, the sports trainer at my school massages the muscle and shows me how to stretch it. The massage definitely helps."—Jen Brill, 17

Natural Remedies Offer a Safe Alternative to Dangerous Prescription Drugs

Chris Sumbs

Chris Sumbs is a writer for Ezine Articles, an online publisher, and is the creator of Underground Health.com, an online source of alternative medicine products and information.

Alternative medicine's day is coming. Natural remedies are helping people from around the world find solutions to their health problems. Drug companies don't like this. Drug companies need people to visit the doctor so doctors can prescribe their drugs and they can make money. A lot of money.

Prescription drugs can be very dangerous. Ironically, many of the substances found in these drugs are natural. When these natural substances are modified and mixed with synthetic additives you get a prescription drug. While they (drugs) treat the symptoms, they can also cause harmful, sometimes deadly side effects. Just look at all of the lawsuits. Prescription drugs can be on the market for several years before people realize just how dangerous they are. By then, thousands of people have consumed them and now have serious health risks. These are the same drugs that were found to be safe by our very own FDA [Food and Drug Administration]. This is ridiculous. It's all about money. I heard a rumor that the FDA receives something like $100 million or more every time they approve a drug. I don't know if this is true, but it would make sense because of how much these big companies charge and earn selling these drugs. Thankfully, we have an alternative ways of solving our health problems. These methods are both safe and effective. I'm referring to what's called Complemen-

Chris Sumbs, "A Safe Alternative to Dangerous Prescription Drugs," in *Ezine Articles*, January 13, 2008. http://ezinearticles.com/?A-Safe-Alternative-To-Dangerous-Prescription-Drugs&id=926103.

tary Medicine. Common names for this type of healing include faith healing, folk medicine, holistic medicine, natural medicine, unconventional medicine, unorthodox medicine.

The Business of Prescription Drugs

I was introduced to natural medicine about five years ago [2003]. I was shocked when I began to research just how dangerous prescription drugs are. Since that time, I have sparingly used pharmaceuticals and try to use only natural remedies. I eat a good diet rich in natural foods including fruits and vegetables. I must admit we do need certain prescription drugs. In the case of terminal illness, certain drugs and treatments may be the only means of preserving life. It is acceptable to have side effects when it comes to life or death. Preserving life is always worth the cost both financially and physically. Other instances where I believe prescription drugs are justified are incurable ailments where strong suppression is required such as HIV.

What I don't understand is how physicians can keep prescribing dangerous drugs that cause severe side effects to people who don't fall into these two categories. Some of these people aren't even sick. I could go into the doctor's office tomorrow, tell them I'm depressed, and they'd give me a prescription on the spot. That very drug may cause side effects far worse than the original ailment. It's unbelievable how easy it is to get a prescription. Doctors all too often are freely writing these prescriptions. Drug companies have admitted to giving gratuities and other "kick backs" to doctors and clinics for prescribing certain drugs. I guess the memo is, "push more of our drug and we'll give you more gifts and financial aid". What . . . is going on here? When I go to the doctor, I want to know he's looking out for me, not his own pocket book! Isn't a healthy six figure income enough? I bet we would all be shocked if we found out what really goes on behind the scenes. It's a business of pushing dangerous drugs on decent people who are looking for honest help. It's unethical and just plain wrong. These drugs all too often cause side effects that are more severe than the condition they are intended to treat.

Wouldn't it be wonderful if [doctors] were looking out for our best interest and not that of the pharmaceutical companies and in some cases their own financial gain?

I have personally experienced the side effects of prescription medication. Years ago, prior to gaining knowledge of alternative medicine, I was prescribed a certain prescription drug for anxiety. I was going through some major life changes, and felt like I needed something to level me off. I went in and confided in my doctor and she gave me a drug called xxxxx. She told me not to worry about side effects or dependency. I trusted my doctor and I took the drug for six months. Bad decision. During that time, I became very detached and very much indifferent about everything in my life. In addition, I gained 50 pounds! I'm not exaggerating. My diet didn't change, I simply added the drug and I went from 180 to 230 lbs. in six months. It took me over 3 years of being off that drug to get back to my normal weight. And then there was the biggest challenge, addiction. I became addicted to it. If you have ever been addicted to a prescription drug you know what it's like trying to wean off it. It was a terrible time in my life. I lost many friends and my family suffered as well. But, with a lot of work and dedication, I overcame my addiction. Fortunately, I was able to recover and today I am 100% healthy and will never use a drug like that again. That experience caused me to have a major attitude adjustment towards prescription drugs and western medicine and really got me involved in holistic healing and natural medicine.

Stop Trusting Big Business

We as a nation have grown up being taught to trust our doctors. We confide in them our most private ailments and rely on them to "fix us". Wouldn't it be wonderful if they were looking out for our best interest and not that of the pharmaceutical companies and in some cases their own financial gain? I don't know if this will change anytime soon, but it will someday. I developed a website that shares some of the natural methods of healing. I encourage you to come and check it out. I've included a health blog on the site and hope people find the information helpful. By sharing knowledge with others, I hope to change the way people look at health and medicine. We need to stop trusting big business, which is always driven by profit, and start using our human instincts and the natural resources of our wonderful earth.

Acupuncture Is Safe and Effective

Emily Laber-Warren

Emily Laber-Warren is a writer for Women's Health Magazine.

Kimberly Adams was training for her first triathlon when she felt a sudden and excruciating pain in her neck. A social worker and mom of two, she suspected that toting around her 7-month-old daughter might have contributed to the injury. Adams saw a doctor, who ruled out a pinched nerve and sent her to a chiropractor. An x-ray showed nothing structurally wrong and the chiropractor made some adjustments, but the pain persisted.

Desperate, Adams, 33, turned to acupuncture. And on her third visit—after 3 weeks of unremitting pain—something radical happened. The acupuncturist wiggled a needle in Adams's calf while massaging the painful muscle in her neck; the neck muscle began to relax, and 40 seconds later it felt better.

"Literally the next day, the pain was completely gone," Adams says.

Adams, of Scotch Plains, New Jersey, has been pain-free since and recently completed her second triathlon. Researchers don't quite understand how a needle inserted into one body part can heal another, and some doctors consider the practice at best a nebulous, power-of-positive-thinking sort of thing. But for the 2 million Americans who are treated annually with acupuncture, recent clinical studies have shown that the practice affects the body in measurable ways—reducing blood pressure, for example, and increasing the circulation of endorphins, natural pain-relieving chemicals.

Emily Laber-Warren, "Special Report: Acupuncture," in *Women's Health Magazine*, January/February 2006.

In 1997 the National Institutes of Health [NIH] approved acupuncture for certain kinds of nausea and pain and listed 11 other conditions, including addiction, asthma, carpal tunnel syndrome, and menstrual cramps, for which it showed potential. Scores of new studies are published each year, evaluating acupuncture's effectiveness in treating everything from Parkinson's disease to depression. And thousands of physicians have incorporated acupuncture into their practices—the country's most prestigious training program, at UCLA's medical school, has graduated 5,000 doctor-acupuncturists over the past 2 decades.

Acupuncture in Chinese Medicine

Acupuncture is based on the traditional Chinese teaching that energy, or qi (pronounced "chee"), courses through the body along channels called meridians; illness occurs when that flow is disrupted. Scientists are starting to identify some of the physiological mechanisms at work, and there's evidence that the insertion of needles into designated acupuncture points speeds the conduction of electromagnetic signals within the body. These signals may increase the flow of endorphins and other pain-relieving chemicals, as well as immune system cells, which aid healing.

But for the patients it has helped, the "why" and "how" it works don't matter as much as the fact that it does.

Nicole Cashman, 33, who heads her own public relations firm in Philadelphia and New York City, had suffered from allergies all her life. But when she fell for a man with two dogs, her problem escalated from annoyance to life crisis. After just minutes at her boyfriend's house, itchy eyes and other painful symptoms would set in, forcing her to flee. An allergy doctor had her try Zyrtec pills, steroidal eye drops, and a prescription nasal spray. The medications quelled her symptoms, but left her with dry eyes, headaches, and intense drowsiness. "I was like a walking zombie," she says.

Cashman's mom, a pediatric nurse practitioner, suggested she try acupuncture. Though nervous, Cashman began seeing Marshall Sager, D.O., for 20-minute sessions every 2 weeks. He treated her with needles in her face, shins, hands, chest, and other parts of her body. Within a month she was off her meds and sleeping over at her boyfriend's. "I've had amazing results," says Cashman, who has been allergy- and medication-free for more than 2 years and now sees Dr. Sager for semi-annual tune-ups. "I consider myself completely cured."

A Visit to the Acupuncturist

I've changed into a flimsy gown and am waiting for the acupuncturist, Phillip Shinnick, Ph.D., to return. I'm here mostly because of frequent sinus infections, but a couple of other things are on my mind—like my jaw, which is tight from grinding my teeth at night, and, given the fact that I've been trying to get pregnant for 7 months, acupuncture's reputation for increasing fertility. The room is casually disheveled, an odd melding of doctor's office (sink and white-tiled floor) and massage studio (Buddha wall art and padded examining table).

Based on my reading, I'm expecting this first [acupuncture] session to start with a medical history and then move in a less traditional direction.

Shinnick isn't a doctor, but he has studied physiology intensely. (Actually, he's done a lot of things intensely. He set the world record in 1963 for the long jump and competed in the 1964 Tokyo Olympics.) He was a history and sociology professor at Rutgers when a car accident led him to seek physical therapy at Robert Wood Johnson University Hospital in New Brunswick, New Jersey. Doctors there sensed his natural gift for healing and suggested he seek training; he went on to study with several top physicians with expertise in Eastern medicine. From there he proceeded to teach acupuncture to doctors at New York Medical College.

Based on my reading, I'm expecting this first session to start with a medical history and then move in a less traditional direction, with him feeling my pulse, examining my tongue, and asking questions like, "What three adjectives would you use to describe yourself?" In traditional Chinese medicine, the world consists of five elements: fire, water, earth, wood, and metal. One or two elements are dominant in each of us, and they're considered a fair predictor of both health issues and psychological tendencies. "It's the feng shui of the body," explains Ann Cotter, M.D., a physician and acupuncturist at Morristown Memorial Hospital in Morristown, New Jersey. A "fire" person and a "metal" person, though they have the same complaint, are likely to receive needles in different places.

But Shinnick merely asks about my principal complaints and medical history, then palpates my whole body, stopping to make marks on a rough human outline he's sketched. I see him circle my shoulders, the left side of my lower back, my left thigh, and both calves. He's done Chinese medical typing, he says, but he finds it more efficient to examine a person's body; all the information he needs resides there.

With a speed that would seem like impatience if he weren't being so attentive, he points out problems.

My stomach and pancreas are in spasm.

My right hip is locked, and it's pressing on my ovary.

I have a scattering of tiny bumps on my cheeks.

"There's congestion in these points," he says. "It's been this way for a long time."

His plan: Two needles in my lower back, two in my shoulders. Another in my abdomen, near my right hip. Tap-tap, tap-tap. I feel microsecond pinpricks, and in some spots, a numb, achy sensation.

Shinnick attaches clips to the needles and starts what looks like a car battery. I feel pulses of electricity alternating from one needle to the next. It feels odd but not uncomfortable, though my abdomen is visibly convulsing. Acupuncturists insert their thin needles, as many as a dozen at a time, into any of more than 300 points. Placement varies from one session to the next, in response to the patient's changing condition, and the practitioner may twist the needles or apply a weak electrical current. I lie there, a reposing pincushion, as Shinnick attends to patients in other rooms, and ponder his comments. At least one of them seems eerily on target. I've felt soreness in my lower-right abdomen for years, and in a recent test I had to make sure my fallopian tubes were clear, the right one was so constricted that the doctor had to force the dye solution through it.

Advocates also point to the fact that acupuncture has virtually no side effects: a well-trained practitioner will use sterilized, disposable needles, eliminating the chance of infection.

Twenty minutes later Shinnick is back. The needles come out, snip-snap. My problems are neatly connected. "To me, everything fits," he says. My stomach is in knots, he explains, which is causing the outbreak on my face. The tension in my shoulders is keeping my sinuses in crisis and contributing to my jaw clenching. The blockage in my hip is hampering my ovary.

"I can completely eliminate all your tension," he says, "but you'll put it back." Unless, that is, I change my habits. He teaches me to breathe deeply into my stomach, relaxing my face on the exhale. "You need to practice these self-care techniques every single day from now until the day you die," he tells me. Most acupuncturists don't expect their clients to work so hard between sessions, but then again most treat patients regularly for weeks or months at a time. Shinnick believes two or three sessions are usually sufficient. "If it's going to work, it'll work fast," he says.

"It's Looney Tunes," says Stephen Barrett, M.D., a retired psychiatrist who operates the Quackwatch Web site. "Meridians and qi are part of a delusional system." Dr. Barrett is referring to the vocabulary of acupuncture. Qi has no counterpart in Western medicine, and the meridians are not visible structures. "It's two worlds," Dr. Cotter says. "It's like learning a new language."

Western doctors treat problems that patients have; Eastern doctors treat patients who have problems. "Western medicine has a tendency to stop or alter processes. Just think about the names of our medicines: antibiotics, antihistamines, interferon," Dr. Sager says. "Acupuncture enhances the body's inherent ability to heal itself."

Acupuncture Shows Promise

Since being validated by the NIH in 1997 for nausea and postoperative dental pain, acupuncture has shown promise for other ailments. In 2004 alone researchers documented its effectiveness in treating at least 25 medical problems. But none of those studies was sufficiently large or well designed to be definitive.

That doesn't mean the studies are wrong, only that they are not the final word. No company stands to profit from the revelation that acupuncture works, so it's hard to fund the large, costly studies that Western medicine requires for proof. In addition acupuncture isn't easily standardized the way Western treatments are—decisions about needle placements change each session based on how the patient is feeling—so it's hard to design an objective study.

Victor Sierpina, M.D., a physician at the University of Texas Medical Branch and author of a recent review of the medical literature on acupuncture, says acupuncture has been shown to work for . . . osteoarthritis of the knee. A 2004 study of 570 patients published in the *Annals of Internal Medicine* showed that those who received acupuncture for 26 weeks scored 33 percent better on tests of pain and joint immobility than did patients who received sham acupuncture.

While definitive proof is scarce, anecdotal reports are not. Dr. Sierpina himself has successfully used acupuncture to help patients with migraine and tension headaches, back pain, irritable bowel syndrome, arthritis, tendinitis, neuralgia, allergies, chronic fatigue, fibromyalgia, asthma, and menstrual cramps. Other doctor-acupuncturists told me they've had results with acute ankle sprains, tennis elbow, male and female infertility, sinus infections, and the common cold. "I hear from patients weeks later, 'I still feel great.' That outcome is demonstrable. It's real," says Elizabeth Huntoon, M.D., a physical medicine and rehabilitation doctor at the Mayo Clinic who is also a certified acupuncturist. "If you have enough patients saying that to you, you start to believe you're doing something right."

Many patients undergo a series of visits over weeks or months before feeling better, or feel some improvement but not a total cure. And there are some who, though their symptoms seem treatable, don't respond to acupuncture at all. No one knows why; some attribute it to acupuncturists with insufficient skills or to individual body differences.

"It may be genetic—specific pain receptors may be diminished in some people," says Brian Berman of the University of Maryland school of medicine, who headed the knee osteoarthritis study. Nonresponders tend to be people who've been in pain for years; and advocates suspect that even they could be helped but that entrenched problems take longer and many patients give up too soon.

A nifty little $200 device by my bed tracks my hormone levels based on urine samples I provide each morning. For the past 7 months, it's been the same drill: a couple days of high fertility before and after ovulation, which for me happens several days earlier than the optimal day 14 or 15, followed by low fertility the rest of the month. But after I start acupuncture, things change. This month I register high fertility for 17 days straight. The downside: I don't ovulate. The upside: Something seems to be shifting inside me.

Acupuncture seems to work best for problems that Western medicine struggles to treat.

I can't help but think of Eliana Jacobs, 42, an acupuncture patient I'd interviewed. She'd had trouble conceiving her first child, but the second go-round was even worse. Over several years she had an ectopic pregnancy that cost her a fallopian tube and four in-vitro fertilization [IVF] procedures at two top fertility clinics in New York City. The doctors found nothing wrong with her eggs, but they failed to develop into sturdy embryos. "After four IVF procedures, which are physically and mentally grueling, I had nothing to show for it," she says.

As a last-ditch effort, Jacobs went to an acupuncturist who specialized in fertility. She was told it could take 3 to 6 months of regular treatments to restore her body to equilibrium. Jacobs decided to give it a try, then do one last round of IVF. She went dutifully twice a week, though she felt no physical difference and had no idea whether acupuncture was working. Six months later though, she found she'd gotten pregnant on her own, and went on to have a second healthy girl.

Was Jacobs's experience mere coincidence? Hard to say. A 2002 German study showed promise for acupuncture in helping women undergoing IVF become pregnant. Eighty women were given acupuncture 25 minutes before and after embryo transfer; another 80 were not. The pregnancy rate of those who received acupuncture was 42.5 percent, as opposed to 26.3 percent for those who didn't.

When Western Medicine Fails

Some of the most interesting research about how acupuncture works involves brain scans. In one of the first such studies, published in 1998 in a prestigious medical journal, *Proceedings of the National Academy of Sciences*, researchers needled subjects on the side of the foot in points that are thought to affect the eyes while taking images of their brains in an fMRI [functional magnetic resonance imaging] machine. The part of the brain associated with vision lit up, just as it did when a bright light was shone in the subjects' eyes. Needling in other parts of the foot did not cause the response.

Acupuncture seems to work best for problems that Western medicine struggles to treat—hot flashes, recurrent infections, back pain, and other chronic conditions that don't register on x-rays or blood tests—not extreme medical conditions. Advocates also point to the fact that acupuncture has virtually no side effects: a well-trained practitioner will use sterilized, disposable needles, eliminating the chance of infection. The worst that patients can expect is some bruising or a brief feeling of faintness. Hence practitioners say acupuncture is a good option when other treatments have failed—or when Western medicine has no answers.

Which is pretty much where I find myself right now. A blood test I recently took indicated that my chances of getting pregnant are low, but the doctor who ordered the test, a fertility specialist, had no remedy to suggest except to wait and take the test again, as results may vary from month to month. Meanwhile my current cycle, the second since I started acupuncture, is the best yet; this time I register high fertility early on, then ovulate on day 15—the ideal scenario.

What it all means for me I don't yet know, but the changes in my body make me feel certain that the acupuncture is doing something. Acupuncture doesn't work for everybody all the time, but it clearly does work for some people some of the time. And I hope I'll be one of them.

Many Alternative Medical Treatments Are Safe If Performed Properly

Consumer Reports on Health

Consumer Reports on Health *is a monthly newsletter published by Consumers Union, publisher of* Consumer Reports *and an independent, nonprofit organization that tests and provides results on all types of products and services for consumers.*

Alternative medicine is starting to emerge from the long, bitter battles between believers and debunkers, often waged in the virtual absence of scientific evidence. Treatments such as acupuncture, massage, guided imagery, relaxation training, therapeutic touch, tai chi, and yoga are now used in clinics and hospitals alongside conventional treatments. Indeed, such methods are now often called "complementary" or "integrative" medicine. Mainstream medical schools offer courses in alternative methods. Most important, alternative therapies are being tested in well-designed clinical trials, and reliable evidence about safety and efficacy is starting to emerge.

Myths About Alternative Medicine

Having confidence in a treatment is more important for alternative remedies than for standard treatments. False. Many aspects of alternative medicine may promote high expectations, such as ample time with the practitioner, attention to the whole person, and the prestige of ancient therapies. But there's plenty of evidence that expectations can shape the outcomes of conventional treatments, too. One classic study of people with asthma found that the effects of both airway openers and constrictors were substantially greater when people were told the real effect of the drug than when they were falsely informed it would have the opposite effect. Moreover, experts we consulted say there's no research to show that mere confidence in alternative methods accounts for their benefits. On the contrary, unconventional therapies have helped even skeptics. And alternative techniques have been more effective than similar "sham" procedures, as in some studies comparing needle placement at real acupuncture points vs. random sites.

Hypnotherapy doesn't work for some people because they're inherently resistant to hypnosis. True. Almost everyone can achieve some form of light trance, such as daydreaming. However, reports suggest that 10 to 20 percent cannot enter the level of trance needed for hypnotic suggestion. In that state of relaxed attention, you're more responsive to suggestions for changing behavior, managing illness, and altering physiological processes. For example, one review of clinical trials concluded that self-hypnosis can reduce pregnant women's use of pain medication by about half. Other research shows that hypnotherapy lastingly relieves symptoms of irritable bowel syndrome in the vast majority of cases. Hypnosis seems to work best when you're highly motivated. If you've tried hypnotherapy unsuccessfully, you may have been unreceptive at the time rather than intrinsically resistant.

[Many] alternative methods . . . rarely cause substantial adverse effects—provided they're performed properly on appropriate patients by qualified practitioners.

Acupuncture needles are painful when they're inserted. False. The hair-thin needles cause little or no pain in most people. However, a needle may occasionally be inserted close to a nerve, causing a sharp twinge. And patients often feel a deep aching sensation; according to traditional Chinese medicine, that happens when the needle hits a channel of vital energy. Most people consider it "a good ache," although some find it unpleasant, says William M. Boggs, M.D., an acupuncturist and medical director of the Center for Integrative Medicine at the University of Maryland.

The vast majority of alternative techniques are virtually risk-free. Mostly true. The alternative methods discussed here rarely cause substantial adverse effects—provided they're performed properly on appropriate patients by qualified practitioners. The one major exception: Avoid chiropractic manipulation of the neck, which in rare cases can trigger a stroke. In addition, take these common-sense precautions: Make sure your acupuncturist uses disposable needles sealed in a sterile package. Avoid massage if you have advanced osteoporosis, nerve or blood-vessel damage, or a clotting or bleeding disorder. Avoid chiropractic treatment of an injured or inflamed joint. And try to choose a therapist certified by a reputable group.

While tai chi can increase flexibility in healthy joints, it can't help joints damaged by rheumatoid arthritis. False. Staying mobile is a major challenge for people with rheumatoid arthritis, since conventional high-impact exercise can cause further damage. Some evidence suggests that tai chi, which features gentle movements, may safely help those people. In two small, 10-week clinical trials, rheumatoid-arthritis patients who did tai chi once or twice a week improved their range of ankle, hip, and knee motion without harmful effects. Another small trial found it reduced pain and swelling. If you have rheumatoid arthritis and want to try tai chi, seek an instructor experienced in teaching people with arthritis. And ask for modifications if a movement or posture is uncomfortable.

Unconventional methods tend to interfere with standard cancer treatments. False. Using an alternative therapy instead of a prescribed cancer treatment can have grave consequences—and certain herbs and supplements can reduce the effectiveness of chemotherapy drugs. But growing evidence indicates that many alternative methods may be safely used alongside standard ones. For example, clinical trials suggest that mind-body methods can quell stress and ease the pain of medical procedures. Massage therapy, now offered in many hospice programs and cancer centers, can lessen anxiety. And acupuncture can minimize the nausea caused by chemotherapy.

While meditation can boost mood, it's not useful if you're prone to depression. False. To minimize the risk of relapse, doctors often advise clinically depressed people to keep taking medication indefinitely. Now a technique that combines mindfulness—an established relaxation method—and cognitive therapy, which tries to eliminate irrational, negative thoughts, may offer an alternative. Mindfulness-based cognitive therapy focuses on the self-critical thoughts that can help cause relapse. This eight-week training program teaches people not currently depressed to recognize negative thoughts and feelings as merely transient mental events. In two one-year studies of people who've had repeated bouts of depression, those who got the training were half as likely to relapse as those given only the usual care by their doctor.

It's wise to have your physician diagnose your symptoms before you seek other treatment.

Spinal manipulation is the best alternative treatment for low-back pain. False. Manipulation is the most frequently chosen alternative treatment for back pain. But it's not necessarily the most effective. Studies of acupuncture, yoga, mind-body methods, massage, and spinal manipulation (usually done by chiropractors) suggest that all offer modest relief. In general they're safer than surgery or drugs and about as effective. In the absence of clear differences, the best therapy may be the one in which you're most confident. Confidence may make you more likely to stick with a treatment, or may yield extra benefits via the placebo effect.

Mind-body therapies may be useful for chronic illness, but not for surgery. False. More and more hospitals are offering mind-body treatments to ease jitters before surgery and promote healing afterward. One review found "strong evidence" that preoperative use of relaxation, hypnosis, guided imagery, and similar methods can reduce pain and speed recovery. Other research indicates that such techniques before surgery—and sometimes during or after—can cut both the risk of postoperative complications and the use of pain medication.

It's not worth telling doctors about alternative treatments since they'll probably be dismissive. False. While some physicians may object to nontraditional methods, it's still essential to try communicating openly about how you're handling any significant physical or psychological problem. Indeed, it's wise to have your physician diagnose your symptoms before you seek other treatment. Your doctor may tell you that the treatment you're considering is ill-suited for your condition or must be modified to avoid harm. The more your physician understands your approach to health, the better the two of you can work together.

Pets Can Be Safely Treated with Noninvasive, Natural Remedies

Victoria Anisman-Reiner

Victoria Anisman-Reiner is a certified aromatherapist, a holistic health practitioner, and a feature writer on natural medicine topics for Suite 101, an online publisher.

People who practice alternative medicine for themselves and their families are often curious about how to apply the same healing techniques to their pets and other animals. Questions arise like: Can I use these essential oils on my budgie? My dog has an infection—is there a natural remedy that can help? Is it true that essential oils can kill cats?

Stories about animals who were successfully treated with natural remedies abound:

- Birds dosed with homeopathic remedies who survived debilitating viruses;
- Dogs who bounce back from digestive injuries after energy work and liver cleansing;
- Horses with colic or broken bones that a vet said would have to be put down, but who pulled through after intensive treatment with essential oils.

Alternative medicine can be just as effective for animals as for humans. However, it's important to remember that natural treatments are potent medicine. We must exercise due caution in using essential oils, herbs, homeopathic remedies, and other natural treatments on our pets, just as we would on ourselves or other people. In fact, it's advisable to take even more cau-

Victoria Anisman-Reiner, "Alternative Medicine for Pets: Safe Use of Aromatherapy, Homeopathy, Herbs & Energy Work on Animals," *Suite101.com*, April 9, 2007.

tion when using remedies on pets, for two reasons: an animal can't tell you how it feels or what hurts; and most animals' sense of smell is very acute.

What Hurts?

Because a dog or cat can't communicate what hurts or what makes them feel better the way a human can, it can be difficult to diagnose an illness or apply treatment to the right place. For this reason, anyone eager to treat their pet with a natural remedy should always have the animal seen by a veterinarian first, so that you ensure that you're using a natural treatment for the right problem.

A vet can also run tests to establish what may be counter-indicated on a particular animal. For instance an older pet with a low thyroid will not do well with wintergreen or willow for pain relief; other herbs and oils should be used instead that won't suppress the thyroid.

Sensitive to Smells—and to Energy

Animals like dogs, cats, guinea pigs, rats, mice, birds, and horses all have an acute sense of smell. This means they may react especially strongly to remedies like essential oils that have a potent aroma. Don't let this discourage you from using your preferred healing techniques on your pets—but *do* be aware that you should use less of an essential oil or herb on a cat or dog than you would on a human.

Treat them as you would a small, sensitive child. Do not apply essential oils or scented lotions or salves on an animal's face unless absolutely necessary. As with a small child, the bottoms of the feet are the safest place to apply essential oils (pets have reflexology points, too!).

This sensitivity often extends to hands-on healing and energy work. Animals can be highly attuned to energies. Be gentle with them, and explain what you're doing and that your intent is only to help. If they react negatively to reiki or energy work, pay attention and back off. Most animals will respond very positively to energy work if we pay attention to their reactions.

Treating pets with non-invasive natural remedies can be a great way to respect their health.

The stories about cats dying from exposure to essential oils are a myth. Anecdotal evidence and personal experience have shown that if you use oils from pure, organic sources that have been distilled at only low temperatures, without solvents, they are safe to use on cats in small measure. Please use extreme caution if you are uncertain of the source of an essential oil or how they have been pressed. *Adulterated oils are not safe.*

Tips and Suggestions

Everyday pet problems tend to respond well to simple natural remedies.

Even a beginner can use homeopathic "Rescue Remedy" cream to treat skin issues on their pets, or use essential oils like Thieves [a combination of oils] to clean up pet odors in the home.

Some of the best natural medicines are preventative:

- Use natural pet shampoo instead of exposing your pet to toxic chemicals;
- Give them a garlic supplement instead of poisonous flea treatment (which have been known to kill cats);
- Feed them all-natural pet food instead of the usual store-bought junk.

Treating pets with non-invasive natural remedies can be a great way to respect their health and everyday wellness as we do our own.

Natural Does Not Mean Safe

Sarah Houlton

Sarah Houlton is a science writer in residence at Cambridge University, as well as a journalist specializing in pharmaceuticals, chemicals, and chemistry.

In the eyes of the consumer, 'natural' means 'safe' where herbal medicines are concerned. But this attitude is fraught with danger. Long before the pharmaceutical industry had even been imagined, herbal medicines were used to try and cure illnesses. In the absence of the clinically tested drugs we rely on today, folklore and old wives' tales were the basis of the treatments, with plants and their extracts featuring large. Recent years have seen a resurgence in interest in traditional herbal medicines: patients equate 'natural' with 'safe', all too often believing that formally tested medicines are artificial and therefore must be unsafe. This thinking is clearly erroneous—but also potentially dangerous. Far from being safe, many commonly used herbal medicines like St John's Wort and ephedra are actually very potent drugs in their own right, with all the implications this has for side-effects. And, most worryingly, they can have potentially serious interactions with prescribed medicines.

There are many culturally different reasons for the popularity of herbal medicines. The recent rapid rise in their use in the US owes a lot to the surge in 'new age' spiritualism. But in Europe—and in Germany in particular—herbal medicines are a part of life, and are even frequently prescribed by doctors; as many as 70% of German doctors routinely prescribe herbal medicines. And most of these are reimbursed by the German health system.

According to Shiew-Mei Huang of the FDA's [Food and Drug Administration] office of clinical pharmacology and biopharmaceutics, nearly 20% of Americans are now taking at least one herbal product, a high dose vitamin, or both. Ginkgo, St John's Wort, ginseng, garlic and Echinacea each make up around 10% of the dietary supplement market in the US. And all can interact with prescribed drugs. 'Herbal-drug interactions can give altered responses to approved drugs, whether therapeutic failure or altered response,' she says.

Existing pharma legislation will be extended to cover traditional herbal remedies, with good manufacturing practice procedures analogous to those for pharma manufacturers being essential.

The US FDA does not regulate herbal products directly; rather, it treats them as foodstuffs with additional requirements. In 1994, the Dietary Supplement and Health Education Act set out a regulatory framework for safety and labelling, adding a requirement that label claims should not be misleading. The US National Center for Complementary and Alternative Medicine at the NIH [National Institutes of Health] supports research into clinical studies.

Australia's Therapeutic Goods Agency has an office of complementary medicine, which assesses the safety and quality, but not the efficacy, of herbal products. And while there is still no single system in Europe yet, one is currently being developed. The UK [United Kingdom] House of Lords Select Committee has expressed concerns that herbal products should be properly regulated and more research carried out. 'There is a clear need for international collaboration to avoid the duplication of research efforts,' says Iain McGilveray of the University of Ottawa in Canada.

Indeed, while Germany is the third largest market for medicines in the world, it is the largest for herbal medicines, with a market worth around £2bn [2 billion pounds sterling] a year. And many of its mainstream pharma companies, such as Boehringer Ingelheim, have subsidiaries devoted to herbal products.

The European Commission's [EC] proposed new rules will control herbal medicines for the first time, much to the alarm of the health food stores such as Holland & Barrett in the UK, which is conducting a campaign against the legislation. The new EC rules are based on those introduced in Germany in the 1970s. Essentially, existing pharma legislation will be extended to cover traditional herbal remedies, with good manufacturing practice procedures analogous to those for pharma manufacturers being essential.

A Need for Formal Clinical Trials

The big difference, however, is the need for formal clinical trials. These are clearly far too expensive for herbal medicine manufacturers, as their products are unlikely to be patentable, hence recouping the cost will be nigh on impossible. Instead, they will be able to use an existing rule that allows a product to be marketed without formal clinical trials as long as the company can show the product has a good safety record over a period of at least 30 years. This will have to include warnings about potential interactions with medicinal products. And practitioners are facing professional self-regulation controls, much in the same way as osteopaths and chiropractors.

Some people taking supplements are at much greater risk of developing adverse reactions than others. The ill are more susceptible to side-effects than healthy people, and environmental factors also have a great bearing. Perhaps the biggest factor is genetic make-up. As with conventional medicines, herbal products are metabolised by various pathways in the body, notably mediated by the cytochrome P450 enzymes, and the composition of these within the body is genetically determined.

The level of risk for most patients is low, but some, especially those taking toxic drugs at the same time, it is much higher. Reactions can include anaphylaxis [a severe, whole-body allergic reaction] and hypotension [abnormally low blood pressure]. But those most likely to take herbal remedies are actually those who are the most ill—yet, all too often, they do not tell their doctor what they are taking, vastly increasing the likelihood of untoward interactions. According to a White House study, as many as two-thirds of cancer patients take some form of herbal remedy. And the rates in AIDS patients are similar.

Several common foodstuffs are implicated in a number of drug interactions, top of the list being grapefruit and Seville oranges.

The big concern, according to McGilveray, is that these patient populations are exposed to many powerful conventional drugs. 'Most worrying is the use of Chinese herbal remedies,' he says. 'The problem is that no one knows precisely what's in them.'

According to Brian Foster of Health Canada's Therapeutic Products Directorate, there are around a quarter of a million species of flowering plants known, and somewhere around a quarter or a half of these have been used at some time for medical purposes. The World Health Organisation puts the figure closer to 80%. 'These products contain all sorts of compounds—carotenoids, monoterpenes, organosulphur compounds, phenolics, tocopherols, triterpenes and so on,' says Foster. 'We started to look at them because someone spotted that drinking tonic water while they were taking zidovudine [an anti-HIV medication] made them feel unwell.'

Health Canada has now investigated almost 200 different natural products to establish levels of actives and the effects they have, including camomile tea, Ginkgo biloba, ginseng, echinacea and feverfew. One might think that all over the counter products contain the same (or at least very similar) levels of ingredients. But, the team found, this is not the case. Growing conditions can have a dramatic effect on the composition of the natural product. The climate makes a difference: humidity, rain, temperature or exposure to frost. And fresh products can be very different from processed ones, which can all too easily lose their volatile oils. Misidentification of plants and substitutions can also be an issue.

Food Stuff Implications

Several common foodstuffs are implicated in a number of drug interactions, top of the list being grapefruit and Seville oranges. While both these fruits contain flavonoids, particularly chrysin, naringenin and quercetin, the culprits for the drug interactions appear to be furanocoumarins, which are also found in celery leaves and lime juice.

These furanocoumarins increase serum levels of several drug products, notably antihistamines, calcium channel blockers and cyclosporin. Statins, buspirone and misoldipine have problems, too.

Mineral supplements can also be problematic. Calcium is essential for bone growth in children, and also in the prevention of osteoporosis, but it can interfere with drugs by intercalation, examples being the antibiotics ciprofloxacin, doxycycline and tetracycline. The interaction between tetracycline and milk was first noted half a century ago. It has since been found that milk can cause a drop in serum levels of tetracycline of as much as 60 or 70%.

St John's Wort [hypericum perforatum] is commonly used as a 'safe' antidepressant, but it can cause a whole gamut of problems. Hypericum perforatum is a perennial with yellow star-shaped flowers native to Europe, where it has been used medicinally for at least 2,500 years, recommended by Hippocrates [Greek physician often called the Father of Medicine]

. . . [and others] for burns, snake bites and fever. It was rediscovered as a medicine in Germany in 1980, where it was approved as a 'safe' antidepressant in 1984, and several clinical trials have shown that it has antidepressant properties.

[The herb] kava kava has been implicated in causing liver damage.

The product is standardised on the ingredient hypericin, despite the fact that it is now known that this is not actually the antidepressant component; hyperforin may act as an SSRI [selective serotonin reuptake inhibitor, a class of prescription antidepressants]. Research at the FDA showed that in the short term St John's Wort had little effect on the major cytochrome P450 pathways, but chronic use selectively induced CYP3A [an enzyme that can interfere with some prescription drugs], particularly in the small intestine.

As a result of this finding, drugs that are CYP3AZ substrates must now contain contraindications to St John's Wort on the label. These include Glivec, and mifepristine. And some St John's Wort products now have to have labelling indicating some of the drugs that can interact.

Kava kava has been implicated in causing liver damage. Kava originated in the Pacific islands, where it is taken in large quantities as a water extract, seemingly without problems. However, the pill product taken as a health supplement contains large amounts of kavalactone, which is essentially absent in the water extract. It is prepared from the root of the pepper plant Piper methyistícum, found in Polynesia, Micronesia and Melanesia. The water-soluble extract does not have the same pain-killing and sleep-inducing properties of the oil-soluble extract in the pills.

However, various reports have appeared in recent years of serious liver problems in patients taking kava products, including cirrhosis, hepatitis and liver failure, in some cases leading to the patient needing a liver transplant. [In 2002], FDA put out a warning letter, saying that great care should be taken, and no one should take kava products without first consulting their doctor. Several countries, including Canada, have removed products containing kava from the market altogether.

Increased Resistance

Another plant whose root is commonly used is echinacea. *Echinacea angostifolia*, which is native to the western US, has purple flowers whose shape led to its common name of the coneflower. The root extract is claimed to increase resistance to infection, and to have aphrodisiac properties. It has been used for centuries in native American medicine, and is now commonly used to ward off the common cold.

The Health Canada team looked at 14 echinacea products, and six biomarkers. . . . Vast differences in components make it very difficult to see precisely what active has what effect, if any.

Garlic, as well as being an important ingredient in cookery, is a common dietary supplement. Yet it too can interact with medicines. A serious adverse interaction was seen in two AIDS patients taking ritonavir.

Both of the hospitalised patients liked garlic, one taking four capsules a day—twice the recommended dose—and the other six or seven cloves of raw garlic. The Health Canada team investigated 10 readily available products, including different lot numbers of the same product, and found very different ingredient profiles.

Geoff Tucker of the University of Sheffield has carried out a large amount of work on drug-drug interactions, including with herbal products. He says that there are a number of special issues that have to be considered with herbal medicines. What are the relevant constituents of the remedy? There can be a very wide variability in their precise composition. The relevant enzymes they affect within the body must be identified. But it's not simple—there are a large number of products and chemicals, and we have no idea what systemic levels people will be exposed to. And there are some special risk groups who will be exposed to much greater amounts.

Tucker is using two approaches. . . . The aim is to evaluate the risk to individuals, and spot patients who are at extreme risk.

They have had some success with drug-drug interactions, such as the interaction between ritonavir and methadone, and Tucker believes that there is no reason why predictions cannot be made for herbal medicines. The only problem is that the composition of the different products can vary so widely—and can vary enormously from batch to batch.

Perhaps Paracelsus [a sixteenth-century physician] had it right. He said that all substances are poisons, and there is none that is not a poison: it is the right dose that differentiates what is a poison and what is a remedy.

The Safety and Quality of Wild Herbs Vary

WHO Drug Information

WHO Drug Information *is a quarterly journal published by the World Health Organization that offers an overview of issues relating to drug development and regulation.*

WHO has published guidelines for good agricultural and collection practices for medicinal plants intended for national governments, to ensure production of herbal medicines is of good quality, sale, sustainable and poses no threat to people or the environment.

Herbal medicines are the natural answer to many ailments and are often locally available. For this reason, their use remains widespread and they are popular in many countries. Because of improved monitoring, reports of patients experiencing adverse reactions with use of herbal medicines are on the rise. Major causes of adverse events can be directly linked to poor quality, particularly of raw medicinal plant materials, or to the wrong identification of plant species. Cultivating, collecting and classifying plants correctly is therefore important.

In addition to patient safety issues, there is the risk that a growing herbal market might pose a threat to biodiversity through over-harvesting of raw materials needed in herbal and traditional medicines and other natural health care products. If not controlled, these practices may lead to the extinction of endangered species and the destruction of natural habitats and resources. The WHO guidelines on good agricultural and collection practices (GACP) for medicinal plants are an important initial step to ensuring provision of good qual-

WHO Drug Information, "Herbal Medicines, Patient Safety and Plant Conservation," vol. 18, Winter 2004, pp. 29–30.

ity, safe herbal medicines and ecologically sound cultivation practices for future generations. The Guidelines cover the spectrum of cultivation and collection activities, including site selection, climate and soil considerations and identification of seeds and plants. Guidance is also given on the main post-harvest operations and includes legal issues such as national and regional laws on quality standards, patent status and benefit sharing.

Safety Issues

The safety and quality of raw medicinal plant materials and finished products depend on genetic or external factors, including environment, collection methods, cultivation, harvest, post-harvest processing, transport and storage practices. Inadvertent contamination by microbial or chemical agents during any of the production stages can also lead to deterioration in safety and quality. Medicinal plants collected in the wild may be contaminated by other species or plant parts through misidentification, accidental contamination or intentional adulteration, all of which may have unsafe consequences. Examples of this are:

- Digitalis: Cases of serious cardiac arrhythmias were reported in the USA in 1997 following the accidental substitution of plantain as a dietary supplement with Digitalis lanata, generally used for heart conditions. Subsequent investigations revealed that large quantities of mislabelled plantain had been shipped to more than 150 manufacturers, distributors and retailers over a two-year period.
- Podophyllum: Fourteen cases of Podophyllum poisoning were reported from Hong Kong, China following the inadvertent use of Podophyllum hexandrum root instead of Gentiana and Clematis species, for their anti-

viral qualities. This accidental substitution arose through the apparent similarity in morphology of the root.

- Aconitum: Cases of cardiotoxicity resulting from the ingestion of Aconitum species used in complementary medicine for acute infections and panic attacks have been reported. Aconitum rootstocks are processed by soaking or boiling in water to hydrolyse the aconite alkaloids into a less toxic, aconine derivative. Toxicity can result when such processes are mismanaged. In the United Kingdom, the internal use of aconite is restricted to prescription only.

Cultivation has replaced wild collection for the supply of some essential drugs used in modern medicine.

The wild type of ginseng (Panax ginseng), used to address digestive conditions resulting from nervous disorders, is currently reported to be rapidly declining due to increasing demand and collection. While wild American ginseng, goldenseal, echinacea, black cohosh, slippery elm and kava kava top the "at-risk list" of endangered species of medicinal plants.

Cultivation has replaced wild collection for the supply of some essential drugs used in modern medicine. The Madagascar rosy periwinkle, Catharanthus roseus, is widely cultivated in Spain and the United States for its properties for treating childhood leukaemia and Hodgkin disease. Demand is also greater than supply for the bark of Pygeum (Prunus africana), a popular natural remedy for prostate disorders in European countries which is harvested from wild trees growing in the mountain forests of continental Africa and Madagascar. Demand is currently unsustainable.

Devil's Claw (Harpagophytum procumbens) is also unsustainably harvested and may become extinct in the wild under current practices. It is used as a tonic, treatment for arthritis and rheumatism, to reduce fever, ease sore muscles, reduce cholesterol, and externally the ointment is used to treat sores, boils, and ulcers. It is also used to cleanse the lymphatic system, and to remove toxins from the blood.

Some Alternative Medicines May Pose Dangers for Kids

Kathleen M. Boozang and Anne Lyren

Kathleen M. Boozang is the associate dean and professor of law at Seton Hall University School of Law. She writes frequently on legal issues implicated by integrative treatments. Anne Lyren is assistant professor of pediatrics at Case Western Reserve University and associate director of the Rainbow Center for Pediatric Ethics at Rainbow Babies and Children's Hospital.

Sophie is a previously healthy five-year-old recently diagnosed with acute lymphoblastic leukemia. Her parents were overwhelmed with fear and anxiety when the possibility of leukemia was first broached by their trusted family doctor, but the doctor, who frequently relies on alternative medicines in his treatment plans, reassured them by pointing out that many successful treatments for cancer exist, including herbal and dietary approaches designed to augment the body's immune system. He recommended these approaches as an alternative to conventional chemotherapy, which he referred to as "human poisons."

The family sought a second opinion from a pediatric oncologist at a nearby tertiary care center. Tests confirmed a diagnosis of acute lymphoblastic leukemia, with a very favorable prognosis. The oncologist explained that a widely accepted chemotherapeutic regimen gave her an 85 percent chance of complete cure. The treatment would take approximately two years, but the initial few months of the treatment would be the worst; likely side effects included nausea, vomiting, hair loss, and mouth sores. She explained that there were medicines available to significantly mitigate these symptoms, and after the initial treatments, Sophie should feel well and continue participation in school and other activities.

The family was reluctant and returned to their family doctor, who again recommended a dietary approach. After anguished discussions, the family decided to try the chemotherapy offered by the oncologist. The chemotherapy put Sophie's leukemia into complete remission during the first few weeks of treatment, but Sophie experienced several of the expected side effects. Although her doctors explained these effects were typical, Sophie's parents were increasingly troubled and returned to their family doctor, who continued to assert that he could treat Sophie's leukemia with a "natural approach" using dietary modifications and vitamin supplementations that he said were proven effective in treating cancer.

The family called the oncologist and explained that they had changed their minds and would be seeking further care from their family doctor. The oncologist consulted with other members of her health care treatment team. They felt Sophie's welfare would be jeopardized if her care were changed. Should they contact the county department of child services to make a report and seek a judicial injunction to allow Sophie to continue to receive conventional chemotherapy?

Alternative Medicines Can Be Dangerous

The question of who should make medical decisions for children is complicated. For the most part, parents have the right and responsibility to act as surrogate decisionmakers for children who have not reached a level of maturity and insight that allows them to act on their own. As children approach adolescence, their capacity to understand the purpose of medical interventions and to weigh risks and benefits is still developing. Our society confers many choices on mature adolescents, but many younger children are not yet able to make complex medical decisions.

The default assumption is that parents are the most appropriate people to make these decisions because they know their children well and are in a position to decide what is in their best interest. But parents do not always make the best decisions for their children. Some children are abandoned, abused, or neglected by their parents. Others have parents whose cultural or religious beliefs lead them to make choices that put the child's life at risk. Our society assumes the responsibility of acting as a watchdog over parental decisions and protecting children from parents who are incapable, unavailable, or reckless. Often, society ensures that children whose health or welfare is significantly jeopardized due to the choices of the parents may be removed from their parents and placed in the custody of the state until a safe environment can be assured. Denying parents medical decisionmaking authority is a dramatic step, but occasionally it is necessary.

Health care providers are often the first to appreciate when a child is being abused, seriously neglected or at risk of grave harm. They are obligated, both morally and legally, to report concerns to the court. The legal system then bears the responsibility for making the most appropriate medical decision for the child. The cornerstone of this decision is fact: all available evidence must be thoroughly evaluated to determine which choice is in the best interest of the child.

No data exists in published peer-reviewed literature that dietary changes or vitamin supplementation is an effective treatment for pediatric leukemia.

Sophie's parents likely acted out of love in choosing an alternative and unproven treatment for their daughter's leukemia, hoping to spare her from the unwanted side effects of chemotherapy. The oncologist's decision should be determined not by the parents' emotions, however, but by available medical evidence. No data exists in published peer-reviewed literature that dietary changes or vitamin supplementation is an effective treatment for pediatric leukemia. On the other hand, the well-documented experience of thousands of survivors of childhood leukemia demonstrates a remarkable chance of assuring Sophie a cancer-free life. Like Sophie, most children experience side effects during the initial phase of their chemotherapy, but the negative long-term impact of such therapy on her quality of life is negligible. The question whether to insist on a medical intervention grows more difficult as the risk of morbidity or suffering increases and the chance of benefit or cure decreases. With an 85 percent chance of cure and treatable and only transient side effects, the promise of benefit undoubtedly outweighs the risk and suffering. Regardless of her parents' ambivalence, standard chemotherapy is clearly in this child's best interest.

Our society has an important role to play in this case: advocating for the best interests of the child. Because children are not the property of their parents, society must impose some limit on parental decisions that are clearly harmful to children or place them at undue risk. The process of reporting, reviewing, and acting in difficult cases represents this duty to children, and the oncologist should initiate this process immediately.

Conventional Medicine More Effective

One of the distinctive characteristics about alternative modalities is that their use is generally precipitated by the patient. Chronically or potentially terminally ill patients and families frequently acquire information about therapeutic alternatives, both legitimate and not, from the Internet. In Sophie's case, however, it is the family's physician who is both recommending and encouraging natural healing methods—not as an adjunct to, but instead of conventional therapy. Exclusive reliance on alternative modalities also deviates from the norm, because most patients integrate non-conventional approaches with the treatment regime recommended by their primary providers, especially when the conventional approach appears very likely to have a favorable outcome, as is the case here.

[Alternative therapy] deviates significantly from the standard of care but also recklessly poses a risk.

The oncologist's first step should be to report Sophie's physician to the state licensing board for pushing the family to pursue a presumably unproven treatment approach that not only deviates significantly from the standard of care but also recklessly poses a threat to Sophie's life. It appears that he has not obtained appropriate informed consent to his natural approach to curing cancer, because he has not informed the family about the empirical data (or lack thereof) regarding his approach as compared with chemotherapy. Neither has he explained that most dietary regimens designed for cancer have their own burdensome side effects and are expensive, time consuming, and unlikely to be covered by insurance. Ideally, intervention by the state licensing board will eliminate this physician as a potential provider for Sophie.

It is premature to contact the county department of child services. Additional counseling should convince the family of the dangers of abandoning chemotherapy. They should be offered an opportunity to develop a treatment plan that safely integrates alternative therapies with those preferred by the oncologist. Many cancer centers have relationships with alternative providers who can work within a treatment plan that is safe and effective for the patient. Alternative therapies might actually ameliorate the side effects and stress caused by the conventional cancer therapy. Further, it sounds as though this family could benefit from counseling to help it deal with the anxieties of Sophie's illness. Alternative practitioners are frequently adored and trusted by their patients precisely because they respond to the holistic needs of the patient—they spend a great amount of time listening to the patient's concerns and identifying ways to ameliorate suffering. This mutual involvement gives the patient and family a greater feeling of control, which is instrumental in patient satisfaction.

If the family resists integration of the two treatment options, the oncologist might consider striking a deal with the family whereby it might employ alternative approaches for a finite period, during which time the oncologist would monitor her condition. If she deteriorates in the slightest, the family would agree in advance to revert to the treatment regime recommended by the conventional providers. This proposal assumes that Sophie would not be placed at any risk by this "trial."

If no amount of bargaining is successful, and the treatment decisions ultimately elected by Sophie's parents present a real danger, the health care team should report the family to the department of child services and seek a court order for appropriate treatment. If at all possible, the parents should not lose custody of Sophie—the court order and state intervention should be limited to ensuring that Sophie gets the treatment she needs to save her life.

Current
CONTROVERSIES

Chapter 3

Are Alternative Therapies Beneficial to Health?

Chapter Preface

The National Center for Complementary and Alternative Medicine (NCCAM) is part of the National Institutes of Health (NIH), which in turn is located within the U.S. Department of Health and Human Services and is the only federal government agency dedicated to providing information and research in the field of alternative therapies. NCCAM was preceded by the Office of Alternative Medicine (OAM), which was established in 1991 to investigate alternative therapies that were outside the scope of conventional medical products and services. The OAM's biggest supporter was Senator Tom Harkin (D-Iowa), who revealed in congressional hearings that his allergies were apparently cured by taking bee pollen—an unproven, alternative therapy. The OAM was replaced in 1998 by NCAAM and made part of the highly respected NIH. As stated on its Web site, NCAAM's mission is to "explore complementary and alternative healing practices in the context of rigorous science, train complementary and alternative medicine researchers, [and] disseminate authoritative information to the public and professionals."

Since 1991, Congress has approved ever-increasing budgets for NCAAM and its predecessor. The OAM began with an annual budget of only $2 million, but by 2002 NCCAM's budget had increased to more than $100 million. Altogether, the federal government has spent more than $800 million to research alternative therapies. Over the years, NCCAM has funded hundreds of scientific projects designed to understand whether and how various alternative therapies work. Among these, for example, are projects to examine the effectiveness of acupuncture therapy; studies to test the subluxation theory of chiropractic care; and clinical trials to evaluate the medicinal effects of popular dietary supplements, such as St. John's Wort, echinacea, and glucosamine. NCCAM claims that this research is gradually building a body of data that is helping to inform the public about alternative therapy options and guide public policy on such issues as regulation of supplements.

However, NCCAM has come under heavy criticism throughout its existence. Many experts in the medical research community say that despite the expenditure of hundreds of millions of dollars, NCCAM has not scientifically demonstrated the effectiveness or safety of any alternative therapy. Rather, critics claim, the agency has funded a host of unscientific studies of highly questionable therapies (such as homeopathy and psychic healing) that have produced only negative outcomes—that is, a lack of evidence that the particular therapy has any positive health effect. And since it takes numerous trials to prove or disprove the effectiveness or safety of any particular therapy, critics claim that the body of research produced by NCCAM to date—which amounts to a spattering of studies on numerous alternative therapies—proves almost nothing and is of very little scientific value. Critics also complain that the NCCAM Advisory Panel, charged with setting the agency's policies and direction, is biased in favor of alternative medicine because it includes many representatives from the various CAM professions. As two prominent doctors and CAM critics, Donald Marcus and Arthur Grollman, succinctly put it in a July 21, 2006, article in *Science* magazine, "We believe that NCCAM funds proposals of dubious merit; its research agenda is shaped more by politics than by science; and it is structured by its charter in a manner that precludes an independent review of its performance."

Supporters of NCCAM counter that while the OAM may have had problems, the 1998 creation of NCCAM within the NIH and the appointment of biomedical scientist Stephen Strauss as its director in 1999 marked a sea change in the credibility of the agency. Strauss, supporters say, promised to study CAM practices according to rigorous scientific principles, and this has produced research studies of higher quality and reliability. Critics remain unconvinced, however, and some have called for NCCAM to be defunded. Only the future will tell whether NCCAM will continue to exist and receive federal funding and whether its research will help to solve some of the questions concerning the effectiveness of CAM products and practices

In any case, the controversy surrounding NCCAM is representative of one of the central issues about alternative therapies—namely, whether they are quackery or beneficial to health. The authors of the viewpoints in this chapter provide further information and present the range of differing views about this important issue.

Alternative Medicine Can Save Lives

Megan Irwin

Megan Irwin is a writer and journalist who lives in Phoenix, Arizona.

Unconventional treatments paid off for 4 desperately ill women. These courageous pioneers faced extreme disability or death. But when they exhausted the best traditional treatments for their diseases, their hope endured. Instead of giving up, they sought—and found—new life on the frontiers of alternative medicine. Along the way, each of the women grappled with fear and uncertainty while coping with the rigorous physical demands of their unproven treatments. But they've all defied their grim prognoses, and live each day filled with energy, optimism, and joy. Learn by their examples what it takes to forge a personal path to your best health.

Raphaela Savino, 68, Brooklyn, Nurse

Then: A diagnosis of stage 2 ovarian cancer. Now: "I've been healthy for 15 years."

As a nurse, Raphaela Savino was always admired for her strength and independence. So it came as no surprise to her friends and family that after she was diagnosed with aggressive ovarian cancer in 1992, she chose an unconventional path toward recovery. Savino did have surgery to remove her ovaries, uterus, and fallopian tubes but refused the recommended follow-up chemotherapy, which promised her a 70% chance of surviving for 5 years. "Having cared for cancer patients, I knew chemo would make me sick and destroy my immune

Megan Irwin, "Alternative Medicine Saved Our Lives," *Prevention*, vol. 59, September 2007, p. 174.

system, which I needed to get strong," she says. If the time she had left was limited, she wanted to pack it with as much joy and energy as possible.

Still, she felt she should do something and became interested in alternative strategies for staving off a recurrence of the disease. Her research led to Nicholas Gonzalez, MD, a Manhattan immunologist who's had success treating cancer with pancreatic enzymes, which come from pigs. Gonzalez's approach is based on century-old research by Scottish embryologist John Beard, who first theorized that enzymes in the pancreas could have strong cancer-fighting properties. Gonzalez prescribed the enzymes and a custom diet consisting of raw foods, vitamins, minerals, and trace elements designed to fight cancer and bolster her immunity, which appealed to her because it was the opposite of what she feared from chemo. The supplements totaled nearly 200 pills a day. "This is really aggressive medicine," Gonzalez says. "We're as tough as any oncologist is with chemo. The idea that you just drink some green juice is not true. It's a tough road."

A Strict Plan

How tough? Savino rose every morning before dawn to prepare her meals, apportion her pills, and plan her detoxification routine, all the while coping with side effects typical of the early stages of the treatment, such as aches and extreme fatigue. "I was exhausted. But I could feel the effects right away, and that made me stick with it. I began to look better, more alive. I felt like my immune system was being challenged in a positive way, not destroyed, like with chemo."

As each month passed, she felt better and stronger. Blood tests revealed an increasingly vigorous immune system and declining cancer markers. Within 18 months, she began reducing the number of supplements she took and today, 15 years later, is down to about 70 pills a day. She hasn't seen an oncologist in that time but is confident she is healthy. "I'm stronger than ever," says Savino, who now also works as a health care consultant. "I take adventure trips—white-water rafting, horseback riding—to Utah and Canada. The younger women are always amazed. They can't believe I had such a serious illness."

Then: Needed a metal rod to support her spine. Now: "I do 10-minute headstands."

Although Savino credits her special diet for warding off a recurrence, the American Cancer Society [ACS] has a different explanation: "The surgery is what saved her life," says Barrie Cassileth, PhD, chief of the integrative medicine service at Memorial Sloan-Kettering Hospital in New York City and an ACS spokesperson. "It's important to eat well and stay strong, but no diet has ever been shown to cure cancer." She points out that the greatest risk in pursuing alternative care for a serious illness is that it may prevent you from receiving lifesaving conventional treatment.

Bottom line: Ovarian cancer is deadly, surgery offers the only proven chance of a cure, and chemotherapy provides insurance. Most doctors would consider Gonzalez's regimen only as an adjunct to conventional therapy.

Kathy Simonik, 52, Barrington, IL, Graphic Designer

Then: Needed a metal rod to support her spine. Now: "I do 10-minute headstands."

After several back operations and years of therapy, Kathy Simonik was advised [in 2002] to have two final surgeries to implant a metal rod running through much of her spine. Although it would drastically impede her range of motion—she wouldn't be able to turn her head without turning her entire body—the procedure, her doctors said, would relieve her incessant pain.

Good Reason to Be Skeptical

Simonik had good reason to be skeptical about the operation's success. Her last surgery, to implant two metal rods and six screws, left her with 18 months of sciatic nerve pain. So she ignored their advice and turned instead toward an obscure alternative treatment called naprapathy. "I left the doctor thinking, I gave this my all. I said no and never went back." She mentioned her decision to a friend, who recommended that she see Patrick Nuzzo, a local naprapath. Naprapathy is a form of manual medicine that, like chiropractic care, focuses on musculoskeletal conditions. "Where we differ from chiropractors is that we don't continually adjust the spine the way they do," Nuzzo explains. "We treat the tissue around it as well. Each vertebra in the spine is supported by 17 ligaments. Tension in those supports causes rigidity, reducing blood flow to nearby tissues. From her degenerative disease and the surgeries, Kathy had decades of tension built up in her spine. My challenge was to release that tension."

Simonik received treatments every 2 weeks and continues to today. Her mobility gradually increased and the intense pain faded. She was able to go off the pain medication she'd taken every day for years. At Nuzzo's suggestion, Simonik began working with a yoga instructor to strengthen her muscles and increase her flexibility. Today, she can do back bends and headstands. "It didn't come easy," she says. "It's taken 4 years. It wasn't hard to be dedicated, because I was in so much pain. I was willing to do anything to stop it. My instructor says the most motivated student is the one who wants to move out of pain and into freedom. I'm a living example."

After three failed back surgeries, Simonik can hardly be blamed for not having another. "I tell my patients to try anything and everything before they resort to an operation," says Noah S. Finkel, MD, an orthopedic surgeon in Huntington, NY, and spokesperson for the American Academy of Orthopedic Surgeons. "The reason she got better was probably because her therapist helped break down all the scar tissue she had and stretched out the cramped ligaments around her spine. The exercises then helped her rehab her muscles and stabilize her pelvis." Finkel says a variety of therapies, including chiropractic and deep-tissue massage, may help back surgery candidates avoid an operation.

Miasa Pasha, 55, Phoenix, Small Business Owner

Then: Bedridden from chronic pain. Now: "I go dancing with friends."

As you watch her shimmy and shake on the dance floor at a local club, you'd never guess that just 3 years ago Miasia Pasha was depressed, discouraged—and in constant agony. HIV positive since 2001, she was taking a cocktail of antiretroviral medication that caused terrible side effects, including pain in her feet that made it impossible for her to walk—not to mention enjoy her favorite recreational activity, dancing. "It was like stepping on hot needles," she remembers. "You can't think when you're in such constant pain. All I did was sleep and watch television. And take more pain pills."

Her doctors told her that the drugs Kaletra, Epivir, and Viread, which prevent the HIV virus from replicating, were causing peripheral neuropathy—damage to nerves that results in severe pain. Pasha was in a nasty bind: Take the lifesaving medication and suffer, or forgo the drugs and die. Optimistic by nature, she believed there had to be another choice and sought help at Phoenix Body Positive, which provides services, including naturopathic medicine, to people with HIV/AIDS. There she met Mark Green, then a resident naturopath.

Green says he sees many HIV patients who have become so discouraged by the side effects from their antiretroviral drugs that they stop taking them. His work at Body Positive focuses on making patients well enough to stick with the regimen—and stay alive. For Pasha, he devised a treatment plan that included injections of vitamins B12 and B6, to improve nerve function, and twice-weekly acupuncture. Although phobic about needles, Pasha embraced the therapy: "I was willing to try anything." After 3 months, she was no longer bedridden and started driving her car again. Biweekly treatments reduced the pain in her feet to an occasional prickling sensation—a small price to pay for being able to tolerate lifesaving drugs. Almost as important, she was able to dance again. The memory of her first venture back onto the dance floor with her friends brings tears to her eyes. "I must have danced to about six records in a row," she says of that night. "I was like, I've got my life back."

Acupuncture is not wacky. It's safe and if it helps, it's wonderful.

Because there is often no cure for neuropathy, it's a prime candidate for alternative treatments. To date, no clinical trials have proven that acupuncture works better than medication for neuropathic pain. "But I have patients who receive acupuncture, which seems to help them," says Todd Levine, MD, codirector of the neuropathy center at Banner Good Samaritan Medical Center in Phoenix. "Acupuncture is not wacky. It's safe and if it helps, it's wonderful."

Brooke Sterling, 38, Scottsdale, AZ, Yoga Instructor/Studio Owner

Then: A lifelong battle with cystic fibrosis. Now: "I lived past my death sentence."

Twenty years ago, as an undergraduate at Pitzer College, Brooke Sterling wandered into a yoga class and was immediately transformed. "It was a profound moment," she says. "I had discovered something that was going to change my life." For Sterling, who has cystic fibrosis [CF], an inherited chronic disease that can cripple the lungs, yoga was more than life altering. It was life giving. When she was diagnosed at the age of 6, life expectancy for CF patients was 11 years. (It has since risen to just 37.) "With each pose, I felt my breathing become easier, my lungs loosen up," she recalls. "Afterward, I felt ridiculously courageous for no apparent reason. And I was at ease about my future."

Now, at 38, with a lifestyle centered on her yoga practice and a custom nutritional regimen to take the place of conventional drugs and protocols she has abandoned, Sterling has blown past her death sentence and shows no signs of losing speed. "Yoga has improved my lung capacity to nearly that of someone without CF, depending on the day," she says.

Her departure from traditional CF therapy stands in stark contrast to the path chosen by her brother, Jordan, who also has CF. Both grew up knowing their horizons were considerably foreshortened; the only known treatment that offers a reprieve for respiratory failure due to the disease is a risky double lung transplant. As his condition worsened in his 20s, Jordan decided to go for the operation and, after several years on a waiting list, received a successful transplant in 2001. After a long recovery (many patients reject the foreign tissues), Jordan, 32, now lives a full and active life.

A few years before Jordan went on the transplant wait list—it took him 3 years to be matched with a donor—his sister, whose condition was also deteriorating, discovered Bikram Yoga, an exceedingly rigorous series of 26 postures done in a 105°F room. "Bikram is the best feel-better pill I have ever experienced," she says. After having a bad reaction to a medication she was taking to clear her lungs, she decided to give up using prescription meds to manage her condition.

Because CF also impairs the pancreas, which makes enzymes that help digest food, the disease leaves victims undernourished. Sterling has long struggled to stay above 100 pounds. To maintain her weight, every morning she "douses" her body with nutrients—a handful of supplements she washes down with a smoothie that may include powdered greens, ginseng, royal jelly, brewer's yeast buds, bee pollen, glutamine powder, and colostrum. That's before her regular breakfast of foods like eggs, mangoes, tomatoes, and pita with hummus. She usually eats another five to seven meals a day, with special enzymes to help her absorb nutrients. Sterling also puts her own natural spin on traditional treatments. Instead of the recommended steroids, she has tried inhaling N-acetyl-cystine, a naturally occurring amino acid that thins mucus, from the nebulizer she uses to clear her lungs.

Some experts consider the lack of natural antioxidants to be a possible factor in the inflammation and infection cycle in [cystic fibrosis].

Today, Sterling owns a yoga studio that is also home to a clinic that offers alternative therapies like acupuncture, massage therapy, and Chinese herbal medicine. With her special diet, she's managed to get her weight up to 115 and has a little fat roll around her middle, which she loves. She's even considering trying to have a baby in the next year. The mere idea of giving life to another makes her think immediately of that first yoga class. "It allowed me to live my life," she says.

Sterling's decision to try to avoid a lung transplant is understandable—only 50% of lung recipients are alive after 5 years. According to the Cystic Fibrosis Foundation, one of her greatest risks was giving up her medications. Standard drug regimens include inhalants to keep the airway clear and antibiotics to fight infection. However, the foundation does approve of a high-calorie diet supplemented with vitamins and enzymes like the one Sterling designed to improve her lung health. Some experts consider the lack of natural antioxidants to be a possible factor in the inflammation and infection cycle in CF, according to James Yankaskas, MD, codirector of the University of North Carolina Adult Cystic Fibrosis Program.

Some Alternative Therapies Have Been Shown to Work

Focus on Healthy Aging

Focus on Healthy Aging is a monthly newsletter from the Mt. Sinai School of Medicine, which focuses on helping people maintain their health and vitality in middle age and beyond.

Just as medical technology is becoming more advanced, an increasing number of Americans—and American hospitals—are turning to complementary and alternative medicine (CAM). Nearly 90 percent of seniors surveyed in the Wave of the Health and Retirement Study said they had used CAM, and a recent survey by the American Hospital Association found that more than one in four hospitals offer some type of CAM. "Hospitals are putting in these CAM facilities to offer a variety of different services and to make it convenient for their patients," says David Zhang, associate professor of Community Medicine and Pathology at the Mount Sinai School of Medicine, and a specialist in Chinese medicine.

Here's what the research has to say about four of the most popular alternative treatments available:

1. *Herbal and dietary supplements.* The evidence so far on the effectiveness of herbal remedies such as echinacea (colds), saw palmetto (benign prostatic enlargement), and St. John's wort (depression) hasn't been overwhelmingly positive. One herbal combination that has shown promise, though, is glucosamine and chondroitin. A 2006 study found that it helped participants with mild-to-moderate pain from knee osteoarthritis. What's more, glucosamine and chondroitin had fewer side effects than other arthritis medications. . . .

Focus on Healthy Aging, "Finding Alternative Treatments That Really Work: These Four Popular Therapies Are Used for Everything from Treating Pain to Preventing Cancer, but Some Are Better than Others," vol. 10, January 2007, p. 4.

Dr. Zhang doesn't recommend herbal supplements to his patients, with the exception of glucosamine and chondroitin for people with mild-to-moderate osteoarthritis. If you do take an herbal remedy, talk to your doctor first. Some herbal products and dietary supplements can have side effects, and could potentially interact with medications you're already taking.

The research on acupuncture has been promising for treating . . . low-back pain, neck pain, chemotherapy-induced nausea, headache, and fibromyalgia.

---

2. *Chiropractic care.* Although some studies have indicated that chiropractic care helps patients find relief from low-back pain, it's difficult to draw any real conclusions because the studies done so far haven't been well designed. . . .

People with mild back pain, or mild-to-moderate spinal arthritis may find relief from a chiropractic manipulation, Dr. Zhang says. But stay away from this treatment if you have a disk problem, severe arthritis, or osteoporosis. Let your primary care physician know before you visit a chiropractor, and choose someone who is licensed.

3. *Acupuncture.* The research on acupuncture has been promising for treating a number or conditions, including low-back pain, neck pain, chemotherapy-induced nausea, headache, and fibromyalgia. The biggest and longest randomized study of acupuncture, which appeared in the December 21, 2004 *Annals of Internal Medicine*, found that the practice relieved pain and improved function in people with osteoarthritis of the knee. And a 2006 study found evidence that acupuncture eases low-back pain. . . .

Acupuncture can be a helpful part of a physical therapy regimen for people with arthritis, knee pain, neck pain, and low-back pain, Dr. Zhang says. To find a licensed acupuncturist in your area, ask your doctor for a referral or contact the American Academy of Medical Acupuncture.

4. *Meditation and relaxation exercises.* Stress has been linked to a number of chronic health conditions, including heart and lung diseases and cancer. Research shows that meditation and deep breathing exercises can reduce stress, and may have a positive effect on these conditions. . . .

To relieve stress, practice meditation or deep breathing for 10 to 20 minutes at a time, once or twice a day. Call your local community center or YMCA to find out if there's a relaxation, yoga, or tai chi class offered in your area. Before starting any therapy, see your doctor, preferably one who understands both medicine and CAM therapies.

Alternative Medicine Can Help Alleviate Pain and Chronic Conditions

Women's Health Advisor

Women's Health Advisor *is a Belvoir Media Group publication, which has served the needs of active enthusiasts in a wide range of interest areas for more than three decades.*

If you've ever reached for herbal remedies to ward off a cold, you're in good company. The most comprehensive report ever issued on the use of complementary and alternative medicine (CAM) in the U.S. finds that 36 percent of adults use some form of CAM. Those most likely to turn to CAM are women, says the National Center for Complementary and Alternative Medicine (NCCAM), and the number of women who use such therapies skyrocket among women diagnosed with breast cancer.

Such therapies can improve quality of life. "Studies have proven that acupuncture can significantly reduce the nausea and vomiting connected with chemotherapy, while massage has been proven to reduce local pain and muscle spasms related to cancer and its treatment," says Mary E. Charlson, M.D., director of Weill Cornell's Center for Complementary and Integrative Medicine.

In a report last June [2006] in the *Journal of Alternative and Complementary Medicine*, experts estimate that 20–90 percent of women with breast cancer use at least one complementary therapy every day. The report finds that breast cancer patients thought "CAM would improve health when used in combination with conventional medical treatments."

"Complementary Medicine Benefits: Many Complementary and Alternative Therapies Help Improve Patients' Quality of Life and Reduce Distress" *Women's Health Advisor*, vol. 11, January 2007, p. 6.

One study of women with locally advanced breast cancer found patients used an average of four CAM modalities simultaneously—such as vitamins, nutritional approaches, mind-body therapies, and traditional Chinese medicine. A February 2006 study concluded that after using CAM, patients were less anxious and depressed and more optimistic that their breast cancer would not prove fatal.

In CAM, complementary medicine is used together with conventional medicine, and alternative medicine is used in place of conventional medicine.

Complementary vs. Alternative

In CAM, complementary medicine is used together with conventional medicine, and alternative medicine is used in place of conventional medicine.

Complementary therapies, such as acupuncture, guided imagery, hypnosis, massage, meditation, and reflexology, are in wide use and have been validated by scientific studies, including clinical trials. Now such modalities are integrated with conventional cancer treatments including surgery, radiation, and chemotherapy. That's why centers such as Weill Cornell's call their services "integrative medicine."

On the other hand, practitioners and centers that solely use the term "alternative" often focus on unproven, unconventional approaches, many promising to defeat cancer by boosting immunity or cleansing the body of toxins. Studies have shown that "alternative therapies used as primary treatment for breast cancer are associated with increased recurrence and death," according to the October 2006 *American Journal of Surgery*.

Many alternative therapies don't work, and patients using them die sooner or have a poorer quality of life, stresses Andrew Vickers, PhD, of the Integrative Medicine Service at the Memorial Sloan-Kettering Cancer Center, who has published several studies on the subject.

Which Ones Work?

According to guidelines from the National Comprehensive Cancer Network, acupuncture is one of the nonpharmacologic modalities recommended for pain. One controlled clinical trial randomized 90 patients to receive either acupuncture or acupressure at correct acupuncture points or at random points. Those who received the treatment correctly reported a 36 percent decline in pain intensity after two months, compared to little change in the control group, according to the *Journal of Clinical Oncology*.

Acupuncture and acupressure can also decrease severe nausea during chemotherapy, says a winter 2006 *Journal of Integrated Oncology* article. Acupressure wristbands alone cut severe nausea by 27 to 32 percent.

Other breast cancer patients being treated with chemotherapy find reflexology effective in decreasing depression and anxiety, says an October 2006 Michigan State University College of Nursing study. Recent studies have also found that mind-body exercises like Qi gong, Tai chi, and yoga are effective in improving cancer patients' quality of life. "When used in conjunction with surgery, chemotherapy, and radiation, which treat the cancer, complementary therapies can treat cancer-related symptoms and treatment-related side-effects," says Dr. Vickers.

After Cancer Treatment

Many patients turn to CAM therapies after their treatment ends, seeking a sense of control, says Dr. Charlson. "Once patients have completed initial treatment like chemotherapy, surgery, and radiation, and they are not going to see their oncologist every few weeks, they feel kind of lost and really struggle to make themselves stronger and healthier," remarks Dr. Charlson.

CAM therapies can improve quality of life, Dr. Charlson found in a 2005 pilot study she conducted. The study involved

60 women with breast or gynecological cancer (in their 40s–70s) who were taught meditation, guided imagery, and problem-solving skills in a 20-week program. After the program ended, the women not only reported a clinically significant improvement in quality of life, but also a reduction in fear, anxiety, and stress.

"What surprises patients is that even after their cancer therapy is largely concluded, they find themselves grappling with ongoing issues of stress, anxiety, distress, and depression," observes Dr. Charlson. "Complementary modalities like meditation and guided imagery hold great promise as tools to address these issues."

Alternative Therapies Can Complement Western Medicine

Matthew Solan

Matthew Solan is a writer, editor, and journalist who contributes regularly to health and fitness publications and is a contributing editor to Fit Yoga, *an alternative health magazine.*

Gone are the days of the single family doctor. Today, Americans seek out multiple experts for their medical care, including practitioners in homeopathy, naturopathy, and Traditional Chinese Medicine (TCM). More than one in three Americans use some form of alternative medicine, according to the National Center for Complementary and Alternative Medicine, and that number is expected to go up. "People either want alternatives to Western medicine or they're out of options," says Harriet Beinfield, coauthor of *Between Heaven and Earth: A Guide to Chinese Medicine*. "Western medicine can't always relieve nagging problems like fatigue, bloating, or insomnia, so people seek alternative means."

Here's what the big three of alternative medicine have to offer. Although they shouldn't substitute for traditional Western medical care, they can often complement it by filling in any gaps.

Homeopathy

The principle: In homeopathy, if your internal energy, or "vital force," is out of balance, problems arise. Homeopathy aims to regulate vital energy to stimulate the body's healing powers. Treatment is based on two major principles: the Law of Simi-

Matthew Solan, "Beyond the M.D.: What Can a Homeopath, Naturopath, or TCM Doctor Do for You? Plenty, If You Know What to Look For," *Natural Health*, vol. 37, September 2007, p. 95.

lars (like cures like) and the Law of the Minimum Dose (less is more). An example of the Law of Similars is the remedy coffee cruda: Derived from coffee (a substance traditionally associated with sleeplessness), it is used in homeopathy to relieve insomnia and hyperactivity. According to the Law of the Minimum Dose, the more diluted a remedy, the more powerful its healing properties. Depending on a problem's severity, formulas may be diluted multiple degrees, like 1:10 (labeled as 1X). Remedies are derived from plants, animals, minerals, and other sources, and are taken as pellets, tablets, powders, or liquids.

Naturopathic doctors (N.D.s) believe the body is capable of healing itself.

What to expect: Practitioners conduct one- to two-hour consultations to get a detailed picture of your health and symptoms. They ask about your occupation, daily routine, eating habits, dreams, and how you react to changes in weather, temperature, and environment. Based on this information, the homeopath creates the remedy and potency that best match your needs. Homeopathic pharmacists prepare the remedies on-site.

Good for: Sinusitis, bronchitis, vertigo, varicose veins, flu, ADHD, and children's ear infections.

Cost and resources: $100 to $300 for a first visit; $50 to $100 thereafter. Visit the National Center for Homeopathy site to find a practitioner who has a Certificate in Classical Homeopathy (C.C.H.).

Naturopathy

The principle: Naturopathic doctors (N.D.s) believe the body is capable of healing itself. They find the underlying obstacles and prescribe remedies to clear the path, including taking a detailed medical history, doing a physical exam, requesting lab tests, and using natural treatments that encompass nutrition, botanical medicine, counseling, supplements, and acupuncture.

What to expect: In the initial hour-plus consultation, you'll be asked about your diet, environment, stress levels, and any mental, emotional, or spiritual concerns. An N.D. may also request x-rays and blood tests.

Good for: Menopausal symptoms, insomnia, treating TMJ [temporomandibular (jaw) joint pain], infertility, back pain, middle-ear infections, and severe allergies.

Cost and resources: $150 to $250 for a first visit. Go to naturopathic.org to find a list of practitioners sanctioned by the American Association of Naturopathic Physicians.

TCM

The principle: TCM is rooted in the balance of yin and yang, two complementary polar forces that require free-flowing qi to maintain equilibrium. When qi is blocked, illness results. Practitioners also believe the body is divided into Organ Networks: Liver, Heart, Spleen, Lung, and Kidney. These networks govern specific tissues, mental faculties, and physical activities by regulating qi. Certain ailments are related to a network (e.g., anxiety is linked to the Heart network).

What to expect: The doctor first examines the condition and color of your skin, tongue, hair, eyes, nails, etc. Your personal and family health history, work and living habits, physical environment, emotional life, and even the sound of your voice are also taken into account to determine where qi is blocked and which organ networks are affected. Imbalances are corrected with acupuncture, acupressure, herbal remedies, and moxibustion, a form of heat therapy where dried mugwort is burned over an inflamed area. Meditation, yoga, and qigong [a deep breathing technique] are also prescribed.

Good for: Asthma, insomnia, lower-back pain, and headaches, as well as symptoms and side effects related to diabetes, chronic pain, HIV, and cancer.

Cost and resources: $40 to $150 for a first visit; $45 to $85 for followups. To locate practitioners, visit the American Association of Oriental Medicine; the National Acupuncture and Oriental Medicine Alliance; and the National Certification Commission for Acupuncture and Oriental Medicine.

Alternative Therapies Are Quackery

Stephen Barrett

Stephen Barrett is a retired psychiatrist from Chapel Hill, North Carolina, who has achieved national renown as an author, editor, and consumer advocate. He operates Quackwatch.com, *a Web site dedicated to exposing quackery in medicine.*

"Alternative medicine" has become the politically correct term for questionable practices formerly labeled quack and fraudulent. During the past few years, most media reports have contained no critical evaluation and have featured the views of proponents and their satisfied clients.

To avoid confusion, "alternative" methods should be classified as genuine, experimental, or questionable. *Genuine* alternatives are comparable methods that have met science-based criteria for safety and effectiveness. *Experimental* alternatives are unproven but have a plausible rationale and are undergoing responsible investigation. The most noteworthy is use of a 10%-fat diet for treating coronary heart disease. *Questionable* alternatives are groundless and lack a scientifically plausible rationale. The archetype is homeopathy, which claims that "remedies" so dilute that they contain no active ingredient can exert powerful therapeutic effects. Some methods fit into more than one category, depending on the claims made for them. Blurring these distinctions enables promoters of quackery to argue that because some practices labeled "alternative" have merit, the rest deserve equal consideration and respect. Enough is known, however, to conclude that most questionable "alternatives" are worthless.

An even better way to avoid confusion is [to] sort methods into three groups: (1) those that work, (2) those that

Stephen Barrett, "Be Wary of 'Alternative' Health Methods," *Quackwatch*, February 10, 2004. www.quackwatch.com/01QuackeryRelatedTopics/altwary.html. Reproduced by permission.

don't work, and (3) those we are not sure about. Most methods described as "alternative" fall into the second group. A 1998 editorial in the *Journal of the American Medical Association* made the same point in another way:

> There is no alternative medicine. There is only scientifically proven, evidence-based medicine supported by solid data or unproven medicine, for which scientific evidence is lacking. Whether a therapeutic practice is "Eastern" or "Western," is unconventional or mainstream, or involves mind-body techniques or molecular genetics is largely irrelevant except for historical purposes and cultural interest. We recognize that there are vastly different types of practitioners and proponents of the various forms of alternative medicine and conventional medicine, and that there are vast differences in the skills, capabilities, and beliefs of individuals within them and the nature of their actual practices. Moreover, the economic and political forces in these fields are large and increasingly complex and have the capability for being highly contentious. Nonetheless, as believers in science and evidence, we must focus on fundamental issues—namely, the patient, the target disease or condition, the proposed or practiced treatment, and the need for convincing data on safety and therapeutic efficacy. . . .

Instead of subjecting their work to scientific standards, promoters of questionable "alternatives" would like to change the rules by which they are judged and regulated.

The "alternative movement" is part of a general societal trend toward rejection of science as a method of determining truths. This movement embraces the postmodernist doctrine that science is not necessarily more valid than pseudoscience. In line with this philosophy, "alternative" proponents assert that scientific medicine (which they mislabel as allopathic, conventional, or traditional medicine) is but one of a vast array of healthcare options. "Alternative" promoters often gain public sympathy by portraying themselves as a beleaguered minority fighting a self-serving, monolithic "Establishment."

The Rules of Science

Under the rules of science, people who make the claims bear the burden of proof. It is their responsibility to conduct suitable studies and report them in sufficient detail to permit evaluation and confirmation by others. Instead of subjecting their work to scientific standards, promoters of questionable "alternatives" would like to change the rules by which they are judged and regulated. "Alternative" promoters may give lip service to these standards. However, they regard personal experience, subjective judgment, and emotional satisfaction as preferable to objectivity and hard evidence. Instead of conducting scientific studies, they use anecdotes and testimonials to promote their practices and political maneuvering to keep regulatory agencies at bay. As noted in a recent *New England Journal of Medicine* editorial:

> What most sets alternative medicine apart . . . is that it has not been scientifically tested and its advocates largely deny the need for such testing. By testing, we mean the marshaling of rigorous evidence of safety and efficacy, as required by the Food and Drug Administration (FDA) for the approval of drugs and by the best peer-reviewed medical journals for the publication of research reports. Of course, many treatments used in conventional medicine have not been rigorously tested, either, but the scientific community generally acknowledges that this is a failing that needs to be remedied. Many advocates of alternative medicine, in contrast, believe the scientific method is simply not applicable to their remedies. . . .
>
> Alternative medicine also distinguishes itself by an ideology that largely ignores biologic mechanisms, often disparage modern science, and relies on what are purported to be ancient practices and natural remedies (which are seen as

somehow being simultaneously more potent and less toxic than conventional medicine). Accordingly, herbs or mixtures of herbs are considered superior to the active compounds isolated in the laboratory. And healing methods such as homeopathy and therapeutic touch are fervently promoted despite not only the lack of good clinical evidence of effectiveness, but the presence of a rationale that violates fundamental scientific laws—surely a circumstance that requires more, rather than less, evidence. . . .

The Placebo Effect

When someone feels better after having used a product or procedure, it is natural to credit whatever was done. This is unwise, however, because most ailments resolve by themselves and those that persist can have variable symptoms. Even serious conditions can have sufficient day-to-day variation to enable useless methods to gain large followings. In addition, taking action often produces temporary relief of symptoms due to a placebo effect. This effect is a beneficial change in a person's condition that occurs in response to a treatment but is not due to the pharmacologic or physical aspects of the treatment. Belief in the treatment is not essential, but the placebo effect may be enhanced by such factors as faith, sympathetic attention, sensational claims, testimonials, and the use of scientific-looking charts, devices, and terminology. Another drawback of individual success stories is that they don't indicate how many failures might occur for each success. People who are not aware of these facts tend to give undeserved credit to "alternative" methods.

The fact that an "alternative" method may exert a placebo effect that relieves symptoms is not sufficient reason to justify its use. Therapy should be based on the ability to alter abnormal physiology and not on the ability to elicit a less predictable placebo effect. Placebo therapy is inherently misleading and can make patients believe something is effective when it is not. Without controlled clinical trials, any treatment that is used could receive credit for the body's natural recuperative ability.

Many "alternative" approaches are rooted in vitalism, the concept that bodily functions are due to a vital principle or "life force" distinct from the physical forces.

Medical "facts" are determined through a process in which hundreds of thousands of scientists share their observations and beliefs. Editors and editorial boards of scientific journals play an important role by screening out invalid findings and enabling significant ones to be published. Expert panels convened by government agencies, professional groups, voluntary health agencies, and other organizations also contribute to this effort. When controversies arise, further research can be devised to settle them. Gradually, a shared set of beliefs is developed that is considered scientifically accurate.

Science assumes that in order to develop a coherent body of knowledge, it is necessary to assume that supernatural powers do not exist or, if they do exist, they do not interfere. If such interference were possible, then all attempts at controlled experimentation would be either impossible or pointless.

Many "alternative" approaches are rooted in vitalism, the concept that bodily functions are due to a vital principle or "life force" distinct from the physical forces explainable by the laws of physics and chemistry and detectable by scientific instrumentation. Practitioners whose methods are based on vitalistic philosophy maintain that diseases should be treated by "stimulating the body's ability to heal itself" rather than by "treating symptoms." Homeopaths, for example, claim that illness is due to a disturbance of the body's "vital force," which they can correct with special remedies, while many acupuncturists claim that disease is due to imbalance in the flow of "life energy" (*chi* or *qi*), which they can balance by twirling needles in the skin. Many chiropractors claim to assist the body's "Innate Intelligence" by adjusting the patient's spine. Naturopaths speak of "Vis Medicatrix Naturae." Ayurvedic physicians refer to "prana." And so on. The "energies" postulated by vitalists cannot be measured by scientific methods.

Although vitalists often pretend to be scientific, they really reject the scientific method with its basic assumptions of material reality, mechanisms of cause and effect, and testability of hypotheses. They regard personal experience, subjective judgment, and emotional satisfaction as preferable to objectivity and hard evidence.

Some "alternative" proponents are physicians who have strayed from scientific thought. The factors that motivate them can include delusional thinking, misinterpretation of personal experience, financial considerations, and pleasure derived from notoriety and/or patient adulation.

"Alternative therapy" is a marketing term that should not be permitted.

Overclaim and Puffery

"Alternative" promoters often claim that their approach promotes general health and is cost-effective against chronic health problems. In a recent article, for example, the American Holistic Association's president claimed that various "basic healthy habits" would "tap a well-spring of physical energy experienced as a state of relaxed vitality." In addition to exercising, eating a nutritious diet, and getting sufficient sleep, the list includes abdominal breathing; taking "a full complement of antioxidants and supplements"; and "enhancing the body's ability to receive and generate bioenergy" through regular acupuncture treatments, acupressure, healing touch, craniosacral therapy, qigong, and several other nonstandard modalities. As far as I know, there is no published evidence that "alternative" practitioners are more effective than mainstream physicians in persuading their patients to improve their lifestyle. Nor have any vitalistic approaches been proven effective or cost-effective against any disease.

National Council Against Health Fraud president William T. Jarvis has noted:

> Some techniques referred to as "alternative" may be appropriately used as part of the art of patient care. Relaxation techniques and massage are examples. But procedures linked to belief systems that reject science itself have no place in responsible medicine. Useless procedures don't add to the outcome, just to the overhead.

Rosemary Jacobs, a consumer activist who operates a Web site that debunks colloidal silver [a suspension of submicroscopic metallic silver particles in a colloidal base that has been used as an alternative treatment for AIDS, cancer, and other diseases], has made some penetrating observations with which I agree:

> "Alternative therapy" is a marketing term that should not be permitted. All the public wants is safe, effective and efficient. They also want objective standards of measurement used to determine what is safe, effective and efficient. There is a general consensus as to what those standards are among scientists and rational people for most therapies. In other words, for most diseases and conditions, experts know what works, what doesn't work, what is unknown and what falls into a gray area—what may work but the jury is still out.
>
> Anyone wanting to practice engineering or architecture has to abide by objective standards. I think that anyone who wants to practice medicine professionally should have to do so too. People who believe that personal experience is the best way to evaluate drugs and therapies should have to identify themselves as spiritualists or New Age religious

practitioners but not as medical practitioners. They should be forced to admit to themselves and to the world that they reject science and objective standards, and they should never be allowed to sell the drugs they prescribe.

The NIH Debacle

Many news reports have exaggerated the significance of the National Institutes of Health (NIH)'s Office of Alternative Medicine (OAM). Creation of this office was spearheaded by promoters of questionable cancer therapies who wanted more attention paid to their methods. Most of OAM's advisory panel members have been promoters of "alternative" methods, and none of its publications have criticized any method. In 1994, the OAM's first director resigned, charging that political interference had hampered his ability to carry out OAM's mission in a scientific manner. In 1998, Congress upgraded OAM into an NIH center with an annual budget of $50 million. Today the agency is called the National Center for Complementary and Alternative Medicine (NCCAM) and has an annual budget exceeding $100 million.

When OAM was created, I stated: "It remains to be seen whether such studies will yield useful results. Even if some do, their benefit is unlikely to outweigh the publicity bonanza given to questionable methods." In 2002, Wallace I. Sampson, editor of the *Scientific Review of Alternative Medicine* summed up what has happened:

> It is time for Congress to defund the National Center for Complementary and Alternative Medicine. After [more than] ten years of existence and over $200 million in expenditures, it has not proved effectiveness for any "alternative" method. It has added evidence of ineffectiveness of some methods that we knew did not work before NCCAM was formed. . . . Its major accomplishment has been to ensure the positions of medical school faculty who might become otherwise employed in more productive pursuits.

Alternative Medicine Is Ineffective by Definition

Telegraph.co.uk

Telegraph.co.uk *is the online version of a London newspaper published by Telegraph Media Group.*

Towards the end of [March 2004], there were two health scares. Coca-Cola announced that it was temporarily withdrawing its new brand of purified and bottled water, Dasani, after it was found to contain slightly elevated levels of bromate, chronic exposure to which has been linked with cancer. And at the European Breast Cancer Conference it was revealed that as many as 70 per cent of British breast cancer patients are compromising their chances of survival by using alternative remedies which either do not work or are actually harmful.

There are no prizes for guessing which of the two scares gained the most media attention. In an age when big business is increasingly viewed as a conspiracy against the environment and human health, the sight of a multinational drinks company humbled into removing its products from supermarket shelves was judged to make the more appealing story. Moreover, several newspapers have invested heavily in 'expert' columnists to expound the virtues of mistletoe seeds and shark cartilage; perhaps it is understandable that they should not want to undermine their good work with a front page splash on the hazards of alternative therapies.

As the late John Diamond eloquently explained in his book *Snake Oil*, the life of a cancer-sufferer these days is a constant stream of false hopes: lotions, potions and energy beads which promise salvation without pain but whose claimed benefits have failed to stand up to empirical scrutiny. Many cancer-sufferers go to their graves still believing in the various herbal preparations they have taken religiously throughout their illness. The fact that devotees of alternative therapies have a tendency to die rather more quickly than those who accept conventional treatment goes largely unspoken.

Far from Harmless

In recent years, proponents of alternative medicine have subtly attempted to cover up its shortcomings by rebranding it "complementary medicine", suggesting that just because you want to try a herbal remedy doesn't necessarily mean you have to give up your chemotherapy. In some ways this has made matters worse. One of the most alarming revelations to emerge from [the aforementioned] conference on breast cancer was the number of patients who do not tell their doctors they are taking an alternative therapy on top of a conventional one, and who do not know that the two can react badly with each other.

As argued [at the conference] by Edzard Ernst, a professor of complementary medicine at the Peninsula Medical School in Plymouth [England], alternative medicine is by definition ineffective. Conventional medicine is entirely pragmatic and draws constantly from natural sources. If a herbal remedy shows any sign of effectiveness, it will quickly be subjected to controlled medical trials. Should the alleged benefits of the remedy stand up to this thorough examination, it will be readily adopted by conventional medicine. Alternative medicine is what is left of herbal remedies after conventional medicine has cherry-picked the winners.

For a long time, doctors tolerated alternative therapy as a harmless eccentricity. Increasingly, however, alternative medicines are proving to be far from harmless. To take but one example, [in 2002] the US Food and Drug Administration was moved to issue a warning that kava kava, a popular South American herbal remedy for insomnia and menopausal symptoms, can cause severe liver damage.

Had kava kava been a conventional medicine, there would have been Panorama programmes [a popular UK investigative TV series], petitions, class actions in the courts. Instead, kava kava was discreetly removed from health store shelves and remains available through dozens of websites. Our columnist Christopher Booker is right to point out today that the EU [European Union] regulations governing herbal supplements are hopelessly complex. But we take respectful issue with his claim that products such as kava kava are safe.

That the public should apply different standards of expectation to alternative medicine than they do to conventional medicine is pure Luddism.

That the public should apply different standards of expectation to alternative medicine than they do to conventional medicine is pure Luddism. It is to believe that natural is necessarily superior to synthetic, that the pre-industrial societies (from which come many alternative therapies) were intrinsically wiser than our own. The difference between cancer-sufferers who shun conventional medicine and the Luddites who took to smashing machines in the early industrial age is that today's non-believers in progress tend to be drawn from the higher social classes and they include, as we have said before, the heir to the throne [Prince Charles].

It should be no surprise that users of alternative medicine are relatively well off. Conventional medicine in Britain is free to the consumer at the point of delivery. Alternative therapies, by contrast, are often highly-priced; it is hard to believe that the little pots of herbs lining the shelves of health stores do not sell for profit margins greater than those available on conventional drugs. That alternative medicine has itself become a big business seems not to worry those who have an innate mistrust of pharmaceutical giants. In the public's attitude to medicine, blind belief has taken over from common sense.

Naturopathy Is a Pseudoscience

Barry L. Beyerstein and Susan Downie

Barry L. Beyerstein is a biopsychologist at Simon Fraser University in Burnaby, British Columbia, Canada. Susan Downie is a professor at Carleton University in Ottawa, Ontario, Canada.

Naturopathy is the most eclectic of "alternative" practices. It has changed its methods in response to popular fads and beliefs. It practices no pool of consistent diagnostic or therapeutic methods. The most notable things that unite its practitioners are a penchant for magical thinking, a weak grasp of basic science, and a rejection of scientific biomedicine, which they refer to as "allopathy." Because naturopathy lacks a coherent rationale, patients can encounter anything from commonsense lifestyle advice—eating a healthy diet, rest, exercise, and stress reduction—to an array of scientifically implausible nostrums and gadgets.

A Mystical Foundation

If a glue binds the diverse and changing patchwork of naturopathic practices together, it is espousal of the teachings of the early nineteenth-century romantic movement known as *Naturphilosophie*. The central tenet of this movement affected the romantic poets and artists of the era and some noted scientists as well—that there is a single unifying force underlying the entirety of nature, one that steers all of its parts into a harmonious and indivisible whole. Much like the concept of "Qi" in Chinese philosophy and medicine, this mystical force is said to permeate all living things. Believers in Traditional Chinese Medicine (TCM) assert that imbalances in the flow of

Barry L. Beyerstein and Susan Downie, "Naturopathy: A Critical Analysis," *Naturowatch*, May 12, 2004. www.naturowatch.org/general/beyerstein.html.

Qi are responsible for disease, fatigue, etc., and that that balance between yin and yang variants of Qi is essential to health. Acupuncture, Chinese herbs, etc., supposedly restore well-being by rebalancing the flow of this spiritual essence. Naturopaths explain what they do by resorting to similar metaphorical usages of the terms "balance," "harmony," and "flow," which in the final analysis boil down to synonyms for "good" and have no science-based meaning. The similarities of their theories may explain why TCM is taught in naturopathic colleges.

Although naturopathy uses scientific terms and assumes some of the trappings of science, it exhibits more features of pseudoscience and has magical and quasi-religious roots.

A corollary of *Naturphilosophie* is that in order to comprehend nature one must experience it as a whole—i.e., intuitively rather than objectively and analytically. Openness to one's subjective feelings is considered the most reliable means of revealing the workings of the natural world. Not surprisingly, then, naturopathy has been quick to ally itself with the "holistic health" movement. This emphasis on "holism" helps explain the apparent indifference and/or antipathy of most naturopaths to objective, scientific research.

Naturopathy views sickness as a generalized breakdown of the body in response to "unnatural" events in the environment that can be remedied by overall strengthening of the body's resistance. This clashes with scientific biomedicine's view that disease is a malfunction due to specific pathogens or processes that involve identifiable organ systems. Biomedicine tailors its treatments to the system and pathologic processes that are involved, whereas naturopathy claims to "treat the whole person."

Although naturopathy uses scientific terms and assumes some of the trappings of science, it exhibits more features of pseudoscience and has magical and quasi-religious roots. Its claim that healing stems from a supernatural "life force" is much like the abandoned principle from prescientific biology known as *elan vitale*. Biologists once believed that a force that distinguished living from inanimate matter was derived from a cosmos whose natural order was governed by moral laws—as opposed to the mechanistic ones of modern science. For proponents of naturopathy, "natural laws" are not generalizations from observation and experimentation, but seem to be the moralistic dictates of an anthropomorphic "Nature"—usually capitalized to emphasize its purposeful, theistic properties. They also postulate that health is awarded or withdrawn in accordance with one's ability to maintain harmony and balance with the animistic, vital forces of the universe. In committing itself to vitalism, naturopathy puts bodily functions outside the realm of physics, chemistry, and physiology. . . .

How Do Naturopaths Detect Disease?

Naturopathy's "energies" and "vibrations" cannot be detected by scientific instruments. Most naturopaths use unsound diagnostic and therapeutic devices based on these dubious "life forces." Naturopaths also defend "applied kinesiology," a pseudoscientific technique for diagnosing "toxicities" by subjectively assessing muscle weaknesses allegedly precipitated by refined sugar, food additives, and even fluorescent overhead lighting. In the mid 1970s, an Australian government Committee of Inquiry concluded that a majority of naturopaths used iridology—a diagnostic technique based on the notion that pathology anywhere in the body signals its presence through signs in the iris of the eye. We have found that most naturopaths looking for spiritual energies defend *Kirlian photography* as a diagnostic tool. However, this process, which spiritualists have long believed allows the human aura to be photographed, has a simple, normal physical explanation—a coronal discharge is created in the gas molecules surrounding animate or inanimate objects that are placed in a high-intensity electric field. This discharge is recorded by a conventional photographic process and has not been shown to have any diagnostic value.

Some naturopaths rely on "radiesthesia," which is a form of dowsing. The naturopath passes a pendulum around the patient's body and watches for deviations that pinpoint the site of a problem. One practitioner told us that he likes to use a capsule of an antibiotic as the weight for his pendulum because, being a "bad substance," the antibiotic would "resonate" in proximity to diseased organs. Dowsers and radiesthesiests do not recognize the fact that their own unconscious muscle contractions move the pendulum.

The practices we encountered in our survey of [naturopathy] ranged from the generally supportable to the improbable to the disproved.

Naturopaths state that their remedies are spiritual as well as physical. The Trinity School of Natural Health offers a Doctor of Naturopathy degree to anyone with no prerequisites on completion of 12 correspondence modules. Its promotional literature states: "The school makes no apology for its stance on issues of faith, such as the creation and nature of man, the resurrection, eternity, or any other subject which does not lend itself to double-blind studies, scientific duplication or investigation, but are essential to the spiritual aspect of the whole person." The practices we encountered in our survey of the occupation ranged from the generally supportable to the improbable to the disproved. The list includes: "natural" herbs and nutritional supplements, biofeedback, relaxation techniques, acupuncture, . . . massage, enemas, water baths, heat treatments, aromatherapy, fasting, hypnosis, reflexology, joint manipulation, "realignment" of the cranial bones, bioenergetics, breathwork, magnetic healing, homeopathic potions, therapeutic touch, faith healing, copper bracelets for arthritis, and various Ayurvedic [Indian] and Native-American healing practices. One naturopathy home page we visited recommended wearing socks chilled with ice water to "tone up the immune system" and its operator admitted practicing crystal "healing." These treatments and diagnostic aids are ineffective or unproved. Some naturopaths we interviewed laughed at certain items in the list but embraced others that had even less credibility. . . .

Is Naturopathy a Pseudoscience?

[Philosopher and physicist Mario] Bunge has provided a useful checklist for recognizing pseudosciences. While naturopathy would qualify on almost all of Bunge's criteria, four are especially noteworthy. They are paraphrased in the numbered statements below.

1. Pseudosciences are stagnant, preferring to perpetuate unquestionable dogma from the past rather than progressing as new knowledge emerges from intellectual ferment, debate, internal criticism, and above all, new research. When ideas do change in pseudosciences, they do so in a cosmetic way and usually in response to popular fashions rather than empirical research.

In this electronic age, one might expect an organization's page on the World Wide Web to extol its newest theories and latest scientific breakthroughs. Visiting the Web page of the Canadian Naturopathic Education and Research Society, however, we found instead reverence for the past . . . [including support for] Stanford Claunch, whose ideas date back to the earlier part of the century. Claunch was a founder of "polarity therapy," which claims that numerous diseases result when an alleged left-right electrical polarization of the body becomes disordered. This is treated by the naturopath intuitively "synching" with the patient's "energy field" and laying on of hands to correct the "imbalance." Claunch also advocated "craniosacral therapy," which contends that this energetic imbalance stems from misalignment of the skull bones which must be manually forced back into a healthy configuration. Ninety-five percent of the population allegedly suffers from cranial misalignment. Of course, in the adult, the cranial bones are fused and not "adjustable." Moreover, no competent electrophysiologist has ever detected the electrical fields postulated by Claunch. Undaunted, his supporters still claim that movements of the cranial bones cause movements in the sacrum and vice versa, offering further avenues for therapeutic manipulation. . . .

Very little naturopathic research has been published in peer-reviewed scientific journals.

In 1997, after . . . contacting the Canadian Naturopathic Education and Research Society and the Bastyr University Research Department in person, we had to conclude that research from naturopaths in support of their practices is still a promissory note. They were able to point to virtually none of the core empirical findings, institutionalized review processes, refereed granting procedures, rigorous methodologies, etc., that typify a legitimate scientific enterprise. Pressed for details of the research mentioned on Bastyr University's Web page, their spokesperson, Carlo Calabrese, indicated that their primary efforts to date had been surveys of user satisfaction that employed such subjective yardsticks as patients' self-ratings of their "quality of life." He said a large study was under way that would survey a sample of HIV-positive patients who use "alternative" treatments. Because almost all were also receiving conventional biomedical care and there seemed to be little attempt to control for such confounds, it was unclear how they could determine what would cause any differences in their measures. Concerted efforts to get several other naturopathic associations to steer us to scientific research that supports their premises produced only a handful of references from legitimate journals testing the efficacy of certain herbs. There was nothing to support the associations' eccentric beliefs about nutrition or any of the fringe therapies discussed earlier. The evidence naturopaths themselves presented was almost entirely composed of anecdotes and personal testimonials. In our own search of the relevant scientific literature, we found no compelling support, but we did find other results from empirical evaluations that question the value of the "holistic" approach of naturopathy.

Very little naturopathic research has been published in peer-reviewed scientific journals. In 2003, the *Journal of the American Medical Association* published a study which found that echinacea was no more effective than a placebo in treating children with upper respiratory infections. It now appears that naturopathy's academic community can do some significant research, but how much the outcome of well-designed studies will influence naturopathy's flawed theories and irrational practices remains to be seen.

Based on Untestable Hypotheses

2. Pseudosciences exhibit a general outlook that countenances immaterial entities and processes and untestable hypotheses that are accepted on authority rather than on the basis of logic and empirical evidence.

Radionics, polarity therapy, and therapeutic touch are a few of the naturopathic standbys that postulate immaterial "energy" fields that legitimate scientists cannot detect. Homeopathy, too, posits subtle "vibrations" to explain how pure water can "remember" in order to produce the effects of molecules it no longer contains. As we have seen, naturopathy is thoroughly vitalistic, riddled with unique but undetectable forces and concepts of flow and balance that cannot be empirically tested. Naturopathic "mission statements" we encountered typically repeated the "spiritual" nature of healing.

3. Pseudosciences are isolated from relevant areas of science that they ought to learn from and contribute to. Bogus sciences have little interaction with and are often proud of their isolation from authentic sciences whose findings bear on their claims. Pseudosciences avoid contact with disciplines with which they ought to interact on a regular basis.

It is telling that naturopathy has always had to establish its own colleges to teach its philosophy and practices because no reputable institution of higher learning has been willing to issue naturopathic degrees. As we have seen, naturopaths practically never do research that could be accepted by conventional biomedical journals. Nor is the occupation affiliated with any of the academic umbrella groups (such as the American Association for the Advancement of Science, the U.S. National Academy of Sciences, the Learned Societies of Canada, or the British Royal Society) that promote cooperation and sharing of information among specialized disciplines.

4. Pseudosciences promote hypotheses that are contradicted by an overwhelming body of data from legitimate fields of research.

Clients drawn to naturopaths are either unaware of the scientific deficiencies of naturopathic practice or choose to disregard them on ideological grounds.

Applied kinesiology, radionics, craniosacral manipulation, homeopathy, are examples of dubious practices that clash with scientific knowledge. Similarly, naturopaths, who pride themselves on being specialists in nutrition, typically espouse the unfounded claims propagated by the "health-food" industry. Scientifically trained dietitians have documented the isolation of naturopathy from mainstream science in this regard. The Australian commission, referred to earlier, found that naturopaths in that country were disseminating potentially dangerous nutritional advice such as the avoidance by children younger than five years old of all sources of protein. Naturopathic publications assert that "natural" vitamins (e.g., vitamin C from rose hips) are better for one's health than the identical molecules synthesized on the chemist's bench. A magical orientation is apparent in the off-heard slur that manufactured vitamins must be bad because they are derived from "coal tar." This is equivalent to arguing that a house constructed of recycled bricks from a brothel will be inferior to one built of bricks from a demolished church.

If naturopathy is so poorly validated, why would seemingly well educated therapists and their clients accept such antiscientific approaches to medicine? There are many cognitive biases that can lead both purveyors and purchasers to think that bogus therapies are beneficial. A historical tradition and habits of mind have contributed to the will to believe such practices. These include errors of causality and misattribution (thinking a treatment causes improvement because it precedes the improvement), the power of ritual (physical applications, supplement taking), and suggestion. Curiously, surveys show that naturopaths' clientele are above average in earnings, suggesting a relative advantage in education as well. In addition, the distribution is skewed in favor of female over male clients. . . .

Nostalgia for a Bygone Age

We therefore conclude that clients drawn to naturopaths are either unaware of the scientific deficiencies of naturopathic practice or choose to disregard them on ideological grounds. Naturopathy seems to appeal to magical thinking in people with nostalgia for a bygone "Golden Age" of simplicity when things moved at a more leisurely pace—a halcyon world that probably never existed. Despite the scientific shortcomings of the occupation, there continues to be considerable satisfaction among clients. In addition to benefiting from the placebo effect, many find their sociopolitical outlook nurtured by naturopaths' antiestablishment, antitechnology stance, and others find reinforcement for their faith in a benevolent, human-centered universe. Naturopaths also attract people who, for one reason or another, have been dissatisfied with their contacts with biomedicine. They appeal to people with illnesses with a strong psychosomatic component and those who have chronic conditions for which biomedicine, at present, can offer little. Naturopaths' elaborate history-taking and prolonged "hands-on" interactions provide the human contact and social support that, perhaps unknowingly, many of the so-called worried well are really seeking. They also cater to those with exaggerated fears of side effects of standard medical treatments.

To their credit, naturopaths emphasize the benefits of a healthy lifestyle, the value of prevention, and the desirability of using the least intrusive intervention that will do the job. However, their means of achieving these ideals leave much to be desired while fostering scientific illiteracy in the process. Like most pseudoscientific systems, naturopathy offers [only] comfort to its adherents.

CHAPTER 4

Should the Government Regulate Alternative Therapies?

Chapter Overview

Insight Journal

Insight Journal *is an online resource for people suffering from anxiety- and depression-related illnesses.*

The FDA [Food and Drug Administration] is proposing stricter regulations for herbs, vitamins, vegetable juices and even "devices" such as massage oils, massage rocks, and acupuncture needles under a new guidance document up for review.

CAM Therapies

Complementary and Alternative Medicines are defined by NCCAM (the National Center for Complementary and Alternative Medicine, a branch of the National Institutes of Health) as any medical practices that are distinctly different from those used in "conventional" or "allopathic" medicine generally practiced in the United States. It's a very broad definition, encompassing such practices as acupuncture, massage therapy, herbal supplementation, and aromatherapy.

Use of CAM therapies has risen substantially over the last few years, with one third of adults reporting using some form of CAM in the last year.

According to the document produced by the FDA, use of CAM therapies has risen substantially over the last few years, with one third of adults reporting using some form of CAM in the last year [2006–2007]. Interestingly, the docket also reports that visits to CAM practitioners outnumber visits to primary care physicians each year.

Alarm in the CAM Community

The FDA claims that their regulations are simply a "guidance" as to what constitutes regulated CAM items. The CAM community disagrees. They see the defining of regulated items as an attempt to control the use of CAM within the United States—and possibly incorporate CAM devices and medicines into what some refer to as "Big Pharma," the pharmaceutical industry.

The guidance document essentially defines any item used to treat, mitigate, cure or prevent a disease as regulated by the FDA. This means that if someone claims their vegetable juice helps cure cancer, the FDA then has the right to regulate that vegetable juice as a drug. It also means that if someone is using massage rocks as part of their therapy for a disease or disorder, those massage rocks are regulated as medical devices.

The fear is that, if the FDA declares massage rocks, herbs, vitamins, juices, and acupuncture needles as "drugs" or "medical devices," the same thing will happen for CAMs.

What impact does that have on the CAM practitioner and consumer? If something is regulated by the FDA as a drug or medical device, its use is restricted. People will no longer be able to legally grow or distribute herbs in their garden if those herbs are used for medicinal purposes or administer juice if that juice is said to have health benefits.

This might seem rather inconsequential, but rising drug costs cause alarm within the CAM community. FDA regulations of prescription medication have served a beneficial purpose—but they've also given control of prescription medications to the multi-national pharmaceutical companies, downgrading competition and sending drug costs soaring. The fear is that, if the FDA declares massage rocks, herbs, vitamins, juices, and acupuncture needles as "drugs" or "medical devices," the same thing will happen for CAMs, and consumers will lose their access.

Alternative Therapies Should Be Held to the Same Safety and Competency Standards as Conventional Medicine

Mary Ellen Schneider

Mary Ellen Schneider is a senior writer for Skin and Allergy News, *an independent newspaper for dermatologists.*

Complementary and alternative therapies should be held to the same standards as conventional treatments, according to a new report from the Institute of Medicine [IOM]. "Complementary and alternative medicine [CAM] use is widespread and here to stay," Stuart Bondurant, M.D., said at a press briefing sponsored by the institute. "The same rules should apply for testing of effectiveness and safety regardless of the origin, whether CAM or conventional medicine."

Popularity of CAM Therapies

The use of CAM therapies amounts to $27 billion a year in out-of-pocket costs by U.S. consumers, a figure that is comparable to the projected out-of-pocket expenditures for all U.S. physician services, the report said. In a 1997 survey, total visits to CAM providers (629 million) outpaced total visits to all primary care physicians (386 million). But despite increasing use of CAM services, few patients are disclosing their use of CAM therapies to their physicians. Less than 40% of CAM users told their physicians about their use of alternative therapies, according to surveys in 1990 and 1997.

The IOM committee defined CAM broadly as encompassing "health systems, modalities, and practices and their ac-

Mary Ellen Schneider, "Safety, Efficacy Testing of CAM Needed," *Internal Medicine News*, vol. 38, February 15, 2005, p. 2.

companying theories and beliefs, other than those intrinsic to the dominant health system of a particular society or culture in a given historical period." The definition also states that CAM includes resources that patients perceive as being associated with positive health outcomes.

Licensing boards and accrediting and certifying organizations should set competency standards for appropriate use of both conventional medicine and CAM.

Although the same principles should be used in evaluating both conventional and alternative treatments, some new testing methods may have to be devised for CAM therapies, said Dr. Bondurant, interim executive vice president and executive dean of Georgetown University Medical Center in Washington. For example, randomized controlled trials may not be appropriate for all CAM treatments. Other innovative designs include preference trials that include randomized and nonrandomized arms; observational and cohort studies; case-control studies; studies of bundles of therapies; studies that account for placebo or expectation effects; and attribute-treatment interaction analyses.

The committee recommended educating physicians and other health professionals about CAM therapies. CAM treatment should be addressed in medical school curricula and CME [Continuing Medical Education] courses. Training programs can present CAM information in a way similar to how they addressed areas such as geriatrics and HIV/AIDS over the last decade, said committee member Florence Comite, M.D., of Yale University, New Haven [Connecticut].

Licensing boards and accrediting and certifying organizations should set competency standards for appropriate use of both conventional medicine and CAM, the committee said. CAM practitioners should be involved in research and in developing practice guidelines for CAM therapies, the committee recommended. "The intent of the report is not to medicalize or co-opt CAM but to sustain the existing forms of validated CAM therapies whether integrated into conventional practices or continuing as freestanding approaches," Dr. Bondurant said. "The committee urged that great care be taken to test CAM therapies in the ways that they are actually used."

The report also calls on Congress and other federal agencies to amend the Dietary Supplement Health and Education Act of 1994 to strengthen quality control, accuracy and comprehensiveness in labeling, enforcement actions for misleading claims, and consumer protection, the committee said.

Regulation of Alternative Medicine Is Necessary, but Only After More Research

Edzard Ernst

Edzard Ernst is a professor of complementary medicine at Peninsula Medical School, Universities of Exeter and Plymouth, in the United Kingdom, and editor in chief of the journal Focus on Alternative and Complementary Therapies.

Governments have a legal, moral and ethical duty to protect the public from harm. Since the 'Thalidomide disaster' [thalidomide is a tranquilizer used in the 1960s that was found to cause birth defects], strict regulations are in place to minimise the risk of further medicines-related harm. However, therapist-based areas of medical care such as surgery, psychotherapy and physiotherapy are often more complex to regulate. A degree of control is usually achieved through regulating the healthcare professionals rather than the medicine. With few exceptions, this system has served us reasonably well.

In CAM [complementary and alternative medicine], regulation is in its early infancy. Today, about 20,000 to 40,000 non-medically trained clinicians practise CAM in the UK [United Kingdom]. Dozens of professional bodies for CAM practitioners exist but membership is not compulsory. Thus, anyone could set up as an acupuncturist, herbalist, homoeopath, etc., regardless of their background, training or experience. (The only notable exceptions in the UK are chiropractors and osteopaths who are now regulated by statute.) Realising that this situation is far from optimal, several initia-

Edzard Ernst, "Regulation of Complementary and Alternative Medicine," *Focus on Alternative and Complementary Therapies*, vol. 8, 2003, pp. 291–292. www.medicinescomplete.com/journals/fact/current/fact0803a02t01.htm.

tives aim to change it. The Prince of Wales Foundation for Integrated Health, for example, lobbies for regulating the CAM professions in the UK. Its Chief Executive, Michael Fox, recently stated that 'regulation is first and foremost about protecting patients'.

Proper regulations must include the adoption of accepted ethical standards, such as informed consent. The obligation to obtain informed consent exists for all clinicians and means that, before therapy can commence, patients understand the essentials about it and voluntarily agree to it. Patient autonomy renders informed consent an important prerequisite, particularly when therapeutic risks are involved. The principles of obtaining informed consent are now moving towards warning the patient of all material risks inherent in the proposed treatment, irrespective of the standards of current clinical practice. Chiropractors acknowledge this need: 'where there is a risk of significant harm from the treatment proposed, this risk must be disclosed, understood and accepted by the patient. Such informed consent is required for ethical and legal reasons. The best record of consent is one that is objectively documented (e.g. witnessed written consent or videotape)'.

The creation of an evidence base has to come before, not after, regulation of CAM.

Regulation must also include the obligation of continued professional development (CPD) for CAM practitioners. Like all medical practitioners, CAM providers will need to be aware of the best scientific evidence for or against their therapy: For which indications is CAM effective? What are the risks? At present, 'CPD is uncommon in all CAMs'.

The House of Lords [one house of the British Parliament] recommended that 'CAM practitioners . . . build up an evidence base with the same rigour as is required of conventional medicine . . .' and that '. . . every therapist working in CAM should have a clear understanding of the principles of evidence-based medicine and healthcare'. But what if the best evidence for a given CAM modality is not positive?

Research into CAM is still woefully incomplete. For many forms of CAM, we therefore cannot produce reliable risk–benefit analyses. For some, however, we already know enough to provide at least preliminary information. Acupuncture, for example, is safe and effective for nausea/vomiting. Some herbal remedies do demonstrably more good than harm for certain medical conditions. For other forms of CAM, the benefits are not greater than their potential risks. Iridology, for example, is not a reliable method for diagnosing medical conditions, and chelation therapy is not effective for treating coronary heart disease or peripheral vascular disease. For the vast majority of CAM interventions, however, the balance of risk and benefit is as yet unclear—either because data are too incomplete or contradictory.

A Potentially Serious Conflict

The need for regulation has the potential for creating a potentially serious conflict. Informing patients about the best scientific evidence will, in some cases, mean telling them about the lack of scientifically proven benefit and the presence of potential risks, yet this would be overtly contrary to the personal (financial) interests, beliefs and emotional attitudes of CAM practitioners.

One solution would be only to use therapies for which the best available evidence is positive (i.e. more benefit than placebo and negligible risks). Complementary and alternative medicine providers are likely to oppose this move. It would be a loss to patients that, in their view, experience benefit from other treatments, if only through a placebo effect. They would also argue that it would outlaw treatments for which a large body of historical data implies safety and effectiveness but which are not yet backed up by scientific evidence—absence of proof is not proof of absence! Moreover, this solution would put thousands of CAM practitioners out of work, which might amount to a political and economic impossibility.

It seems that regulation of CAM has 'mountainous obstacles' yet to overcome. The Chief Executive of The Prince of Wales Foundation for Integrated Health insists that 'complementary medicine won't be taken seriously without it', thus disclosing that the motivation behind regulating CAM could partly be the hope for recognition and equality. However, 'fundamental to gaining equality, of course, is presentation of a convincing demonstration of the efficacy of their therapies'—to put it bluntly, regulation of nonsense will still be nonsense. The conclusion is as simple as it is unpopular: the creation of an evidence base has to come before, not after, regulation of CAM.

FDA Regulation of Dietary Supplements Should Be Strengthened

Committee on the Use of Complementary and Alternative Medicine by the American Public

The Committee on the Use of Complementary and Alternative Medicine by the American Public was created by the Institute of Medicine (IOM) to study alternative medicine in the United States; IOM is a nonprofit organization chartered as part of the National Academies of Science that provides science-based advice to the government on issues of science, medicine, and health.

Approximately one-third of adults in the United States use complementary and alternative medicine (CAM) yet less than 40 percent disclose such use to their physician and other health care providers. Women are more likely than men to use CAM therapies; use appears to increase as education level increases; use patterns vary by race, depending on the type of CAM therapy considered; and those who use CAM generally use more than one CAM modality and do so in combination with conventional medical care. Some forms of CAM are being incorporated into services provided by hospitals; covered by health maintenance organizations; delivered in conventional medical practitioners' offices; and taught in medical, nursing, and other health professions schools. Insurance coverage of CAM therapies is increasing and integrative medicine centers and clinics are being established.

What do patients and health professionals need to know to make good decisions about the use of health care interventions, including CAM? Of primary importance is determining that they are safe and effective. Cost-benefit and cost-effectiveness may be important to both the individual and to society. . . . [The Committee on the Use of Complementary and Alternative Medicine by the American Public] has recommended that the same principles and standards of evidence of treatment effectiveness apply to all treatments, with the understanding that certain characteristics of some CAMs and some conventional medical interventions make it difficult or impossible to conduct standard randomized controlled trials. For these therapies, innovative methods of evaluation are needed as are measures and standards for the generation and interpretation of evidence.

Ideally, potential new treatments [would] go through a series of scientific challenges that, if met, lead to acceptance of the test or treatment and integration into clinical practice.

The committee believes that it is necessary and desirable to use a variety of study designs to research CAM therapies. Given the limited funding, the committee suggests that the following criteria be used when considering the CAM therapies to be selected for testing. No intervention will meet *all* criteria, and a therapy should not be excluded from consideration because it does not meet any one particular criterion, for example, biological plausibility.

- A biologically plausible mechanism for the intervention exists, recognizing that the science base on which plausibility is judged is a work in progress and that potential science bases for some CAM therapies have not been well studied scientifically.
- Research could plausibly lead to the discovery of biological mechanisms of disease or treatment effect.

- The condition is highly prevalent (e.g., diabetes mellitus).
- The condition causes a heavy burden of suffering.
- The potential benefit is great.
- Some evidence that the intervention is effective already exists.
- Some evidence that there are safety concerns exists.
- Research design is feasible and likely to yield an unambiguous result.
- The target condition or the intervention is important enough to have been detected by existing population surveillance mechanisms.

Scientific Challenges

Ideally, potential new treatments go through a series of scientific challenges that, if met, lead to acceptance of the test or treatment and integration into clinical practice. Many CAM therapies and many conventional medical therapies, however, are already in widespread use without such validation. The committee therefore concluded that, in addition to research aimed at determining efficacy and uncovering mechanisms of action, research aimed at investigating what is occurring in practice (that is, effectiveness) is also needed. This report proposes that such research be conducted within a research framework with four major components: practice-based research networks, a sentinel surveillance system, CAM research centers, and input from national surveys.

To ensure that research reflects as much as possible the actual ways in which CAM therapies are practiced, it is important to have CAM practitioners involved. However, most CAM practitioners do not have research training. CAM institutions focus primarily on training for practice; research training is rarely a part of CAM curricula. Investments in such training are crucial.

The widespread use of CAM therapies has implications not only for research but also for the education of conventional health care professionals. Health care professionals need to be informed about CAM and knowledgeable enough to discuss with their patients the CAM therapies that their patients are using or thinking of using. However, there are no guidelines for what should be taught, and there is great variation in the content and the methods currently in use. Suggestions for what to teach frequently emphasize critical thinking and evaluation of therapies as well as understanding of different belief systems. Although the content and organization of an individual educational program on CAM will vary from institution to institution, it is important for the health care professions schools to incorporate sufficient information about CAM into their curricula to enable licensed health care professionals to competently advise their patients about CAM. Furthermore, advances in understanding and applying CAM that derive from basic or clinical research should be incorporated into the pre-professional and continuing education programs of all relevant health professionals.

An evidence-based approach to health care delivery . . . [can incorporate] the best options from all sources of care, be it conventional medicine or CAM.

The committee chose to examine more closely the area of dietary supplements because they not only are a prominent part of American popular health culture but also present unique regulatory, safety, and efficacy challenges to consumers, researchers, and practitioners. The committee is concerned about the quality of dietary supplements in the United States. There is little product reliability. Reliable and standardized products are necessary for the conduct of research on safety and efficacy as well as consumer protection, and the committee recommends that the U.S. Congress amend the Dietary Supplement Health and Education Act of 1994 (DSHEA) to require the appropriate reliability of dietary supplements.

The committee believes that the goal should be to provide comprehensive care that is based on the 10 rules outlined in the Institute of Medicine report *Crossing the Quality Chasm*. A comprehensive system uses the best available scientific evidence on benefits and harm, recognizes the importance of compassion and caring, encourages patients to share in decision making about their therapeutic options, and promotes choices in care that can include CAM therapies when appropriate. Scientific inquiry into little understood or unproven ideas, no matter whether they are from CAM or conventional medical sources, can lead to new information that in turn can lead to improvements in care for the public.

Health care is in the midst of an exciting time of discovery, a time when an evidence-based approach to health care delivery brings opportunities for the incorporation of the best options from all sources of care, be it conventional medicine or CAM. The challenge is to avoid parochial bias and to approach each possibility with an appropriate degree of skepticism or belief. Only then will it be possible to ensure that informed, reasoned, and knowledge-based decisions are being made.

Regulation of Alternative Therapies Would Serve No Purpose

Alice Miles

Alice Miles is a regular columnist for the Times *of London.*

The quacks are marching up Whitehall [the road leading to the British Parliament building]. After five years, and the deliberations of a House of Lords [one house in the British Parliament] committee, two government working groups and the Prince of Wales [Britain's Prince Charles], ministers are poised to regulate acupuncture and herbal medicine. A consultation document published [March 2, 2004,] proposes a self-regulation scheme under the umbrella of a complementary and alternative medicine council.

A Bad Idea

What this will achieve is as vague as the health benefits of herbal medicine. The damage it will ultimately do could be devastating. Ministers claim regulation will safeguard the public against dubious products and dodgy docs. Yet alternative medicine does little if any harm. There is the occasional case where a patient refuses conventional treatment in favour of complementary medicine, and dies. But herbal remedies have been shown to be dangerous only rarely. Between 1968 and 1997, the World Health Organisation collected 8,985 reports from 55 countries of adverse incidents associated with herbal medicines, a tiny fraction of the number of adverse events associated with conventional drugs over the same period. Women have been treated in hospital after being prescribed Chinese herbal slimming remedies containing a drug linked to

Alice Miles, "Alternative Medicine Is Too Silly to Regulate," *The Times*, March 3, 2004. www.timesonline.co.uk/article/0,,1058-1023568,00.html.

hypertension and heart disease. Well, more fool them. Ban one quack recipe and these people would take another. You cannot regulate for silliness. And shelling out 50 [pounds sterling] for a pile of wood shavings and some grey-green powdered thing from the local Chinese quack is plain silly.

Why should—how can—government [regulation of alternative medicines] protect [users] against their silliness?

Herbal remedies, along with psychoanalysis, reflexology, aromatherapy and the rest, are the leisure activity of choice for those with too much time and money. Britons spend £1.6 billion [approximately 3.2 billion dollars] a year on alternative medicine.

Why should—how can—government protect them against their silliness? The government proposal says "a modern statutory regulatory framework provides reassurance that a practitioner is not only suitably qualified, but also competent and up to date with developments in practice". Since when? Lawyers are self-regulated but there are corrupt lawyers. Doctors are self-regulated and there are some very bad doctors. Self-regulated physiotherapists and osteopaths range from excellent to very, very poor.

But the new council will confer spurious legitimacy upon many dubious practitioners. It will comprise, among others, practitioners of traditional acupuncture, Western medical acupuncture, Western herbal medicine, traditional Chinese medicine and Ayurveda [traditional East Indian medicine]. Question 10 in the consultation document issued by the Department of Health asks: "Would it be possible for the herbal medicine traditions of Kampo [a type of Chinese medicine practiced in Japan] and Tibetan herbal medicine to be individually represented on Council?" Somebody has too much time on their hands.

According to a report [in 2003] from the Herbal Medicine Regulatory Working Group, which recommended the establishment of the council, the British Ayurvedic Medical Council/British Association of Accredited Ayurvedic Practitioners are less than happy with certain elements of the proposals, but "the Ayurvedic Medical Association who are represented on the working group and the Maharishi Ayurveda Physicians' Association who are not . . . have both endorsed the Ayurvedic medicine element of the curriculum". This will be the oddest and most ineffectual regulatory body known to mankind.

Benefits for Alternative Medicine

Yet its very existence will be entirely beneficial for those it "regulates" and disastrous for the NHS [National Health Service, the publicly funded heath care system in Great Britain]. For the so-called regulation of the alternative health market is an important step in a growing movement to make alternative medicine available to everyone, free.

In an article [in 2001] the Prince of Wales, the movement's figurehead, who has been working with the Department of Health, wrote: ". . . alternative medicine should be available to all on the NHS . . . health should be more than the mere absence of disease or infirmity . . . we should strive to ensure that everybody can fulfill the full potential and expression of their lives." Indeed we should. But it is not the job of the NHS. Feeling unfulfilled without a boyfriend? Got the urge to express yourself with a bit of painting? Trot down to the GP [general practitioner] to demand a "painting the soul" art course—for singletons. On prescription.

Even the practitioners of herbal medicine do not pretend to be able to prove that all of it works. Efficacy is hard to prove, they say, because plants are chemically complex and the active constituents are not always known. For this reason, proposed changes to the 1968 Medicines Act, and an EU [European Union] directive, both aimed at regulating herbal medicines, are trying to ensure simply that they are safe, not effective.

When a respected doctor, Edzard Ernst, former Professor in Physical and Rehabilitation Medicine in Hanover and Vienna, became the first and only professor of complementary medicine in Britain, he found that most of the country's unregulated practitioners were implacably opposed to his plans. Why? He intended to discover which remedies worked. Professor Ernst carried out a clinical trial of arnica, one of the most commonly used homoeopathic treatments, for healing bumps and bruises. He found it is ineffectual: it neither reduces pain nor accelerates healing. Thousands of parents would swear otherwise.

In the end, belief in herbal remedies is just that, a faith. You think it does you some good, it probably does. It does little harm. I have used many forms of it myself. Faith, as they say, can move mountains. But as long as it remains a scientifically unproven and unprovable religion, it should have no part to play in the NHS.

FDA Regulation of Alternative Therapies Could Cost Medicare Billions of Dollars

Nutraceuticals International

Nutraceuticals International *is a publication providing coverage and analysis of diet and nutrition issues for the pharmaceutical, vitamin, and health food industries.*

The US Food and Drug Administration [FDA] is preparing new guidelines that threaten new, costly regulation of complementary and alternative medicines (CAM), used by 74.6% of adults at some point in their lives. The FDA guidance would define a product based on its "intended use." If vegetable juice were sold to satisfy thirst, for example, it would not be regulated, while if it were used to treat a medical condition (e.g., dehydration), it would be, comments The Senior Citizens League (TSCL), a non-partisan US group with around 1.2 million members.

Under the guidelines, it notes, all items used for medicinal purposes—including juices, lotions, vitamins and minerals—could become more expensive and less available. As a result, millions of seniors may be forced to choose conventional treatments within the Medicare system instead of CAM paid for at their own expense, costing taxpayers unnecessary billions, TSCL argues.

Bypassing the Rulemaking Process

The FDA proposal, titled *Draft Guidance for Industry on Complementary and Alternative Medicine Products and Their Regulation by the Food and Drug Administration*, will represent the FDA's official thinking on this topic when finalized, but will not become regulatory policy. However, Congressional investigations frequently have found these types of guidance documents to be "intended to bypass the rulemaking process," TSCL says.

Complementary therapies might include aromatherapy to lessen a patient's discomfort during surgery; alternative therapies might include a special diet to treat cancer instead of chemotherapy. According to the National Institutes of Health, 74.6% of adults have used CAM at some point; a 2006 survey finds that close to two-thirds of adults over the age of 50 have used some form of CAM. The Centers for Disease Control and Prevention (CDC) estimated that the US public spent between $36.0 billion and $47.0 billion on CAM therapies in 1997 alone.

"These changes mean that consumers will be less likely to be able to treat themselves without excessive government interference," said Shannon Benton, executive director of TSCL. "Seniors who previously saved money by treating themselves with vitamins, lotions, or protein shakes may now need a prescription—forcing them to bill Medicare for conventional medical treatments, costing the American taxpayer billions of dollars," he added.

If vitamins and minerals were regulated as "drugs," Medicare might be required to pay for those same vitamins and minerals.

TSCL filed comments with the FDA . . . protesting the impending guidance. In these, it wrote: "currently, few CAM approaches are reimbursed by Medicare and are therefore paid out of pocket by the consumer. On the other hand, if vitamins and minerals were regulated as 'drugs,' Medicare might be required to pay for those same vitamins and minerals. Such a simple change in status for CAM theoretically could cost the federal government billions of dollars annually." It added: "Medicare's trustees forecast that the Medicare trust fund will be exhausted by 2019. The FDA's new proposal risks bankrupting Medicare's trust funds even sooner."

"On behalf of its 1.2 million supporters, The Senior Citizens League is advocating for ways to ensure the long-term stability of Medicare," commented Ralph McCutchen, the group's chairman, adding that, "not only does this secret plan threaten to bankrupt Medicare even sooner, but it takes choices away from seniors when they need them most."

FDA Regulation of Supplements Would Violate Americans' Health Freedom

Ron Paul

Ron Paul is a Republican congressman from Texas and was a 2008 presidential candidate. He is also a medical doctor who practiced obstetrics/gynecology before being elected to Congress.

Millions of Americans take dietary supplements every day, and the numbers are growing as the Baby Boom generation ages. More and more Americans understandably are frustrated with our government-controlled health care system. They have concluded that vitamins, minerals, and other supplements might help them stay healthy and less dependent on the system. They use supplements because they can buy them freely at stores and research them freely on the internet, without government interference in the form of doctors, prescriptions, HMOs [health maintenance organizations] and licenses. In other words, they use supplements because they are largely free to make their own choices, in stark contrast to the conventional medical system.

But we live in an era of unbridled government regulation of both our personal lives and the economy, and Food and Drug administration bureaucrats burn to regulate supplements in the same manner as prescription drugs.

The health nannies insist that many dietary supplements are untested and unproven, and therefore dangerous. But the track record for FDA [Food and Drug Administration]-approved drugs hardly inspires confidence. In fact, far more Americans have died using approved pharmaceuticals than supplements. Not every dietary supplement performs as claimed, but neither does every FDA drug.

Ron Paul, "Dietary Supplements and Health Freedom," www.ronpaul2008.com, April 25, 2005.

The FDA simply gives people a false sense of security, while crowding out private watchdog groups that might provide truly disinterested consumer information. It fosters a complacent attitude and a lack of personal responsibility among people who assume a government stamp of approval means a drug must be safe, and that they need not study a drug before taking it.

The FDA, like all federal agencies, ultimately uses its regulatory powers in political ways. Certain industries and companies are rewarded, and others are punished. No regulatory agency is immune from politics, which is why the FDA should not be trusted with power over our intimate health care decisions.

The Freedom to Choose Health Care

The real issue is not whether supplements really work, or whether FDA drugs really are safe. The real issue is: Who decides, the individual or the state? This is the central question in almost every political issue. In free societies, individuals decide what medical treatments or health supplements are appropriate for them.

Over the past decade the American people have made it clear they do not want the federal government to interfere with their access to dietary supplements. In 1994, Congress bowed to overwhelming public pressure and passed the Dietary Supplements and Health and Education Act, which liberalized the rules regarding the regulation of dietary supplements. Congressional offices received a record number of comments in favor of the Act, which demonstrates how strongly Americans feel about health freedom.

The FDA simply has thumbed its nose at Congress and ignored the new rules in many instances, by attempting to suppress information about health supplements. But in 1999 a federal appellate court affirmed that the American people have a First Amendment right to such information without interference from the FDA. However, members of Congress have had to intervene with the FDA on several occasions to ensure that they followed the court order.

By cooperating with Codex, the FDA is blatantly ignoring the will of Congress and the American people.

My regular listeners already know about another looming threat to dietary supplement freedom. The Codex Alimentarius Commission, an offshoot of the United Nations, is working to "harmonize" food and supplement rules between all nations of the world. Under Codex rules, even basic vitamins and minerals will require a doctor's prescription. As Europe moves ever closer to adopting Codex standards, it becomes more likely that The World Trade Organization [WTO] will attempt to force those standards on the United States. This is yet another example of how the WTO threatens American sovereignty. By cooperating with Codex, the FDA is blatantly ignoring the will of Congress and the American people.

Organizations to Contact

The editors have compiled the following list of organizations concerned with the issues debated in this book. The descriptions are derived from materials provided by the organizations. All have publications or information available for interested readers. The list was compiled on the date of publication of the present volume; the information provided here may change. Readers need to remember that many organizations take several weeks or longer to respond to inquiries.

Alternative Medicine Foundation, Inc.
PO Box 60016, Potomac, MD 20859
(301) 340-1960 • fax: (301) 340-1936
Web site: www.amfoundation.org

Founded in 1998, the Alternative Medicine Foundation provides information to the public and health care professionals about complementary and alternative health care options and the benefits of integrative medicine. The main goals of the organization are to promote ethical integrative medicine use and ensure that indigenous therapies are not lost in the world of modern health care. The organization's Web site contains links to the information databases *HerbMed* and *TibetMed*, as well as numerous resource guides on general and specific CAM modalities.

American Association for Health Freedom (AAHF)
4620 Lee Hwy., Suite 210, Arlington, VA 22207
(800) 230-2762 • fax: (703) 624-6380
e-mail: healthfreedom2000@yahoo.com
Web site: www.apma.net

AAHF provides advocacy on behalf of health care practitioners and consumers who use complementary and alternative therapies. This organization works to ensure that government regulations do not infringe on these individuals' ability to choose the type of medical intervention they provide or receive. Articles on topics concerning the AAHF as well as information on current issues being pursued by the organization are available on its Web site.

American Chiropractic Association (ACA)
1701 Clarendon Blvd., Arlington, VA 22209
(703) 276-8800 • fax: (703) 243-2593
e-mail: memberinfo@acatoday.org
Web site: www.amerchiro.org

ACA, a professional organization for chiropractors, works to advance understanding and standards of chiropractic methods through lobbying efforts, public relations, increased research, and provision of educational materials. Publications such as *ACA News, Journal of the American Chiropractic Association (JACA) Online, Journal of Manipulative and Physicological Therapeutics (JMPT)*, and *Healthy Living Fact Sheets: Patient Education Pages* provide both professionals and patients with the opportunity to learn more about the benefits of the chiropractic modality.

American Council on Science and Health (ACSH)
1995 Broadway, 2nd Fl., New York, NY 10023-5860
(212) 362-7044 • fax: (212) 362-4919
e-mail: acsh@acsh.org
Web site: www.acsh.org

ACSH provides consumers with accurate information on health- and science-related issues. Through activities such as seminars, press conferences, and coordination with the media, ACSH is dedicated to dispensing nonbiased information regarding such topics as alternative medicine, nutrition, pharmaceuticals, and tobacco. The "Facts and Fears" section of the organization's Web site provides a searchable database of articles published by the organization; additionally, the organization's other topical publications can be browsed and searched.

American Holistic Medical Association (AHMA)
PO Box 2016, Edmonds, WA 98020
(425) 967-0737 • fax: (425) 771-9588
e-mail: ahma@holisticmedicine.org
Web site: www.holisticmedicine.org

AHMA is a professional organization of medical doctors, doctors of osteopathic medicine, and medical students who practice or are studying to practice holistic medicine. AHMA works to aid these individuals in their careers and to provide information for professionals and the public about holistic practices. Physician referrals through the organization's database as well as a guide to choosing a holistic practitioner are available on the organization's Web site.

American Medical Association (AMA)
515 N. State St., Chicago, IL 60610
(800) 621-8335
Web site: www.ama-assn.org

AMA is a professional organization of physicians that seeks to improve the health of all Americans. The organization provides policy guidelines on pertinent issues in health care and provides an opportunity for doctors to collaborate nationwide in addressing the needs of patients. Issues related to CAM, such as the integration of alternative medicine and the use of dietary supplements, have been addressed in various issues of the AMA's leading peer-reviewed jounal, the *Journal of the American Medical Association (JAMA).*

The Bravewell Collaborative
1818 Oliver Ave. South, Minneapolis, MN 55405
(612) 377-8400
e-mail: donor@bravewell.org
Web site: www.bravewell.org

The Bravewell Collaborative is a philanthropic organization with the mission of increasing the use of integrative medicine in health care. With scholarship programs that encourage young medical students to enter the field of integrative medicine, public education through the production of the PBS documentary *The New Medicine*, and leadership awards, the Bravewell Collaborative has been at the forefront of promoting improved health care through the cooperation of traditional and alternative medicines. Detailed information about integrative medicine and its relationship to health care is available on the organization's Web site.

Center for Integrative Medicine, George Washington University Medical Center
908 New Hampshire Ave. NW, Suite 200
Washington, DC 20037
(202) 833-5055 • fax: (202) 833-5755
e-mail: info@integrativemedicinedc.com
Web site: www.integrativemedicinedc.com

The Center for Integrative Medicine is one of just a handful of academic- and medical-center-based complementary and alternative medicine practices in the United States. The center's Web site provides useful links to numerous online sources that provide details about various types of alternative therapies.

Citizens for Health
2104 Stevens Ave. South, Minneapolis, MN 55404
(612) 879-7585
e-mail: info@citizens.org
Web site: www.citizens.org

As a national consumer advocacy organization, Citizens for Health works to ensure that consumers have the opportunity and freedom to choose the type of health care they desire. Through grassroots organization and cooperation with private industry, Citizens for Health promotes the idea that government legislation should always protect the right of individuals to choose their own health services. Past issues of the newsletter, *Healthy News*, are available on the organization's Web site, as is additional information about how individuals can become involved in the Campaign for Better Health.

Committee for Skeptical Inquiry (CSI)
PO Box 703, Amherst, NY 14226
(716) 636-1425
e-mail: info@csicop.org
Web site: www.csicop.org

CSI (formerly, Committee for the Scientific Investigation of Claims of the Paranormal) is an organization dedicated to evaluating "fringe-science" claims using science-based methodology and critical inquiry. Through conferences and publications, CSI encourages skepticism about claims related to such topics as complementary and alternative medicine, as well as the paranormal, until such statements can be proven through objective study. The organization publishes the journal *Skeptical Inquirer*, and previously published articles can be found on the CSI Web site.

Federal Trade Commission (FTC)
600 Pennsylvania Ave. NW, Washington, DC 20580
(202) 326-2222
Web site: www.ftc.gov

FTC is an independent agency within the federal government that seeks to ensure that consumers in the United States receive accurate information about products and services sold to them. Projects and resources such as Operation Cure All have been commissioned by the FTC in order to increase consumer understanding and awareness of health-related claims. Articles and reports concerning complementary and alternative modalities and therapies can be found on the FTC Web site.

Mayo Clinic's Complementary & Alternative Medicine Center
Mayo Clinic, 200 First St. SW, Rochester, MN 55905
(507) 284-2511
e-mail: mayoinfo@mayoclinic.com
Web site: www.mayoclinic.com/health/alternative-medicine/CM99999

The Mayo Clinic is a world-renowned health center dedicated to the diagnosis and treatment of virtually every type of complex illness. Its Web site seeks to empower people to manage their health by providing useful and up-to-date information and tools that reflect the expertise and standard of excellence of the Mayo Clinic. The section of the Web site focusing on complementary and alternative medicine provides information on a variety of alternative therapies, herbs, and supplements, and addresses safety and effectiveness concerns with articles about recent research.

National Center for Complementary and Alternative Medicine (NCCAM)
9000 Rockville Pike, Bethesda, MD 20892
(888) 644-6226 • fax: (866) 464-3616
e-mail: info@nccam.nih.gov
Web site: http://nccam.nih.gov

NCCAM is the branch of the National Institutes of Health responsible for addressing issues related to complementary and alternative medicine (CAM) at the federal government level. The organization focuses on researching alternative health practices, informing professionals and the public about findings, and encouraging the integration into conventional medicine of CAM modalities that have stood up to rigorous testing and have been deemed acceptable for use. NCCAM's Web site provides access to numerous fact sheets on CAM practices, as well as video lectures and information about how to order publications.

National Council Against Health Fraud (NCAHF)
119 Foster St., Bldg. R, 2nd Fl., Peabody, MA 01960
(978) 532-9383 • fax: (978) 532-9450
e-mail: ncahf.office@verizon.net
Web site: www.ncahf.org

NCAHF is a nonprofit consumer protection organization dedicated to providing consumers, health care providers, legal professionals, and legislators with accurate information on the vast variety of health care products and services available today. The organization works to ensure that consumers are afforded sufficient and truthful information about health care choices, enabling informed decision making. NCAHF also lobbies for health-related legislation that protects consumers, and the organization publishes a free, weekly e-newsletter, *Consumer Health Digest.*

Office of Dietary Supplements (ODS)
National Institutes of Health, Bethesda, Maryland 20892
e-mail: ods@nih.gov
Web site: http://ods.od.nih.gov

As an arm of the National Institutes of Health, ODS is charged with strengthening medical knowledge and understanding of dietary supplements by evaluating scientific information, stimulating and supporting research, disseminating research results, and educating the public. The ODS Web site contains fact sheets on dietary supplements as well as information about safety and potential side effects. The office also publishes an electronic newsletter, *ODS Update*, that announces new fact sheets, publications, databases, exhibits and conferences, and contains feature stories on timely projects and initiatives of interest.

Quackwatch, Inc.
PO Box 1747, Allentown, PA 18105
(610) 437-1795
e-mail: sbinfo@quackwatch.com
Web site: www.quackwatch.org

Quackwatch is a nonprofit corporation with the mission of exposing fraudulent practices and philosophies within the health field. Previously a member of the Consumer Federation of America, this organization strives to ensure that all claims and advertising relating to health care products and services are appropriately addressed and analyzed. Quackwatch is also dedicated to analyzing information dispensed on the Internet, thereby advancing the quality of information most often referenced by consumers. Links to topic-specific Web sites run by the organization as well as numerous articles concerning these topics are available on the Quackwatch Web site.

The Richard and Hinda Rosenthal Center for Complementary and Alternative Medicine
Columbia University, College of Physicians and Surgeons
New York, NY 10032
(212) 342-0101 • fax: (212) 342-0100

The Richard and Hinda Rosenthal Center for Complementary and Alternative Medicine is an organization within the Columbia University College of Physicians and Surgeons dedicated to applying scientific methods of testing to alternative modalities. In order to achieve the goal of a more complete integration of CAM therapies into the medical system, the center employs rigorous testing to ensure these therapies are safe and effective, educates medical professionals about the benefits of using CAM in conjunction with their current practices, and provides information for medical professionals on a global scale to increase cooperation in advancing CAM practices. Information about specific CAM modalities as well as information about ongoing research can be found on the organization's Web site.

U.S. Food and Drug Administration (FDA)
5600 Fishers La., Rockville, MD 20857
(888) 463-6332
Web site: www.fda.gov

The FDA is the consumer protection agency of the U.S. Department of Health and Human Services that regulates the food and drug products sold to the American public. Vitamins and dietary supplements are among the products the FDA tests using science-based methods to determine their safety and efficacy. FDA ensures that labels provide information about all ingredients included in the product as well as the product's apparent risks and benefits. More detailed information about the projects of the FDA can be found on the department's Web site.

World Health Organization (WHO)
Pan American Health Organization (PAHO)
Washington, DC 20037
(202) 974-3000
Web site: www.paho.org

WHO, and its regional office PAHO, are international health organizations within the United Nations that are charged with ensuring that individuals worldwide are afforded appropriate health care. WHO works to achieve this goal by promulgating international health policies and programs. Because the majority of the world's populations utilize some form of alternative medicine, WHO provides information on traditional remedies and their potential health benefits. Publications such as the *WHO Global Atlas of Traditional, Complementary and Alternative Medicine* and *Legal Status of Traditional Medicine and Complementary/Alternative Medicine: A Worldwide Review* evaluate the status of traditional and CAM modalities worldwide.

Bibliography

Books

Lise N. Alschuler and Karolyn A. Gazella	Alternative Medicine Magazine's *Definitive Guide to Cancer: An Integrative Approach to Prevention, Treatment, and Healing*. Berkeley, CA: Celestial Arts, 2007.
R. Barker Bausell	*Snake Oil Science: The Truth About Complementary and Alternative Medicine*. New York: Oxford University Press, 2007.
Gerard Bodeker and Gemma Burford	*Traditional, Complementary and Alternative Medicine: Policy and Public Health Perspectives*. Hackensack, NJ: World Scientific, 2007.
Michael H. Cohen, Mary Ruggie, and Marc S. Micozzi	*The Practice of Integrative Medicine: A Legal and Operational Guide*. New York: Springer, 2006.
Committee on the Use of Complementary and Alternative Medicine by the American Public	*Complementary and Alternative Medicine in the United States*. Washington, DC: National Academies Press, 2005.
Edzard Ernst, Max H. Pittler, and Barbara Wider	*The Desktop Guide to Complementary and Alternative Medicine: An Evidence-Based Approach*. New York: Mosby, 2006.

Karen Fontaine	*Absolute Beginner's Guide to Alternative Medicine*. Indianapolis: Que, 2004.
Ronald Hoffman and Barry Fox	*Alternative Cures That Really Work: They've Passed Scientific Scrutiny—Now Discover What These Proven Remedies Can Do for You*. Emmaus, PA: Rodale, 2007.
Elizabeth R. Mackenzie and Birgit Rakel	*Complementary and Alternative Medicine for Older Adults: Holistic Approaches to Healthy Aging*. New York: Springer, 2006.
Mayo Clinic	*Mayo Clinic Book of Alternative Medicine: The New Approach to Using the Best of Natural Therapies and Conventional Medicine*. Chicago: Time Inc. Home Entertainment, 2007.
National Center for Complementary and Alternative Medicine	*The NIH Guide to Complementary and Alternative Medicine: Organized by Both Condition and Therapy*. New York: Welcome Rain, 2008.
Kenneth R. Pelletier	*The Best Alternative Medicine*. New York: Simon & Schuster, 2007.
Paul C. Reisser, Dale Mabe, and Robert Velardem	*Examining Alternative Medicine: An Inside Look at the Benefits and Risks*. Downer's Grove, IL: InterVarsity, 2001.
John W. Spencer and Joseph J. Jacobs	*Complementary and Alternative Medicine: An Evidence-Based Approach*. New York: Mosby, 2003.

James C. Whorton — *Nature Cures: The History of Alternative Medicine in America.* New York: Reed Business Information, 2002.

Periodicals

Kimball C. Atwood — "The Ongoing Problem with the National Center for Complementary and Alternative Medicine," *Skeptical Inquirer*, September 2003. http://csicop.org/si/2003-09/alternative-medicine.html.

Australian Doctor — "Acupuncture a Winner in Low Back Pain," October 5, 2007.

Chain Drug Review — "Vitamin C Provides Diverse Benefits," October 22, 2007.

Claims — "Alternative Therapy Prevalent in Auto Injury Claims," December 2007.

Avery Comarow — "Embracing Alternative Care: Top Hospitals Put Unorthodox Therapies into Practice," *U.S. News & World Report*, January 21, 2008.

Jay Cutler — "Alternative Medicine," *Flex*, September 2007.

Patricia B. Gray — "Is This Man Getting Healthier, or Just Poorer?" *Money*, June 2007.

Leon Jaroff — "Wasting Big Bucks on Alternative Medicine," *Time*, May 15, 2002. www.time.com/time/columnist/jaroff/article/0,9565,237613,00.html.

Deborah Kotz — "The Alternate Route," *U.S. News & World Report*, October 29, 2007.

William Marty Martin and Hugh W. Long — "Complementary and Alternative Medicine: Opportunities and Challenges," *Journal of Health Care Finance*, Winter 2007.

Medical Device Week — "Chili Peppers and Acupuncture Needles Are Pain Relievers," October 19, 2007.

Arati Murti — "Alternatives to Drugs," *Physical Therapy Products*, September 2007.

Natural Foods Merchandiser — "Homeopathy Goes Hollywood," January 2008.

Nutrition Week — "NCCAM Gets New Director," February 4, 2008.

Janet Richardson and Karen Pilkington — "Complementary Therapies in Life-Limiting Conditions," *Nursing Times*, August 7, 2007.

Science News — "Snake Oil Science: The Truth About Complementary and Alternative Medicine," January 5, 2008.

Shape — "Last Month on Shape.com, We Asked You: Should Health Insurance Cover Alternative Treatments Like Acupuncture?" November 2007.

Lisa Stein — "Herbal Essence," *U.S. News & World Report*, June 7, 2004.

Rob Stein — "Alternative Remedies Gaining Popularity," *Washington Post*, May 28, 2004. www.washingtonpost.com/wp-dyn/articles/A61657-2004May27.html.

Sara Dabney Tisdale — "Cleaning Up Misconceptions About Colon Cleansing," *U.S. News & World Report*, September 4, 2007.

Alicia Waltman and Camille Chatterjee — "Alternative Medicine Goes Mainstream," *Psychology Today*, July 14, 2006. http://psychologytoday.com/articles/pto-20000301-000024.html.

Marcus Wohlsen — "Veterinarians Turning to Alternative Treatments for Beloved Pets," *Capper's*, February 2008.

Index

B

C

D

F

G

H

O

P

Q

R

S

T

U

V

W

Y

Z